Faith Without Form
Beliefs of Catholic Youth

E. Nancy McAuley & Moira Mathieson

Introduction
George Gallup, Jr.

Sheed & Ward

To my dear sister, Elinor,
whose faith has always inspired me.
Nance

Copyright © 1986
E. Nancy McAuley and
Moira B. Mathieson

All rights reserved. No part of this book may be reproduced or transmitted in any form or by any means, electronic or mechanical, including photocopying, recording or by an information storage and retrieval system without permission in writing from the Publisher.

Sheed and Ward™ is a service of National Catholic Reporter Publishing, Inc.

Library of Congress Catalog Card Number: 85-63382

ISBN: 0-934134-44-8

Published by:

Sheed and Ward
115 E. Armour Blvd. P.O. Box 414292
Kansas City, MO 64141-0281

To order, call: 800-821-7926

Contents

Acknowledgements	iv
Foreword	v
Introduction	1
1. The Study	4
2. The Students and Their Families	8
3. Values and Priorities	15
4. Sexuality, Marriage and Divorce	30
5. God and Prayer	45
6. Sin	55
7. The Church and Religion	69
8. The Parish Community	91
9. Vocations to the Religious Life	106
10. The Non-Catholic Students	122
11. Conclusions and Proposals	136
Appendix	153
Bibliography	165

ACKNOWLEDGEMENTS

The Catholic University of America contributed significantly to the research by providing in-kind support. Special thanks go to Dr. Edmund D. Pellegrino, President William J. Byron, SJ, and to Dr. Dean R. Hoge.

We appreciate funding for the study from the American Board of Catholic Missions, the McCann Charitable Trust, an individual Bishop, and the Religious of the Sacred Heart.

In a variety of ways, the Advisory Board, chaired by Bishop Ernest L. Unterkoefler, offered insights and suggestions. The members were: Bishops Thomas W. Lyons and Walter F. Sullivan; Monsignor Joseph B. McAllister, former Vice-president of Catholic University; Drs. George Gallup, Jr. of the Gallup Organization, Rita Hass of Harvard, Pat Watson of the University of San Diego, Myron Rosenberg, Manager of the Computer Science Corporation, Robert J. Glaser, M.D., President of the Kaiser Foundation, and Margaret Mahoney, President of the Commonwealth Fund.

Dr. Juanita Reaves and Dr. Richard Engler, social scientists, were engaged to assist in conducting and content analyzing some of the in-depth interviews. Many other writers, researchers, and consultants offered their expertise, among them Drs. Dorothy and Philip Harris, Raimundo Panikkar, Anna Thompson, Jane Schaberg, and Raymond McAuley.

Others deserve appreciation for assistance in editing and typing, particularly Sister Adelaide Cassiday, CSC, Helen Burson, Beth Speck, Julie Lind, and Ellen Ferrara.

We are especially indebted to the five Cardinals and thirty-six Bishops who continued to promote the research throughout each phase. The principals and religious educators in the ten sample schools showed admirable cooperation, as did their students whose enthusiasm lent verve to the project.

FOREWORD

Faith Without Form: Beliefs of Catholic Youth represents an important first step for religious systems. Let the data gathered speak for itself! To seek feedback in an organized way, to engage in human factor data gathering and analysis increasingly characterizes modern organizations seeking relevance. It has not been common among church institutions. Thus, the McAuley and Mathieson action research reported here is innovative.

The authors have the foresight to realize that the world, society, and youth are in the midst of a profound transition. They attempted to document the meaning of these changes in terms of the Roman Catholic church and youth enrolled in their church-related secondary schools. There has always been a gap between such youth and their elders. What these researchers have sought is to narrow the perceptual and communication barriers between the generations by obtaining feedback from seniors enrolled in Catholic high schools of the capitol area of the United States. Their random sample of the Washington Archdiocese, which includes suburban Maryland, comprised a diverse mix of students regarding race, sex, economic class, family background, and academic ability.

The authors and their additional interviewers, Dr. Richard Engler and Dr. Juanita Reaves, confronted a common complaint of the young by actually "listening" to what these teenagers have to say about religion, morality, and the Roman Church. They then analyzed and distilled the messages being so conveyed. A review of the interviewers' work shows that the results reported in this text are truly representative. Many may be surprised by the investigators' findings. Others will be so disturbed by the messages coming from this sampling of youth that they may wish to castigate the messengers! That would be a pity, for the research results offer insights and opportunities for renewal of Catholic education and for relevance on the part of parents, teachers, and Church leaders. The findings provide a basis for dialogue with young people enrolled in the independent schools under Church auspices, and for planned change in their school curriculum and methodology. Those who financially supported this research are to be congratulated.

Since churches are also human institutions formulated to serve human needs, this McAuley and Mathieson research approach is most significant. It creates a prototype which should be expanded and replicated. It is a beginning — the methodology of this study could be extended to other diocesan school systems and related subject matter. More importantly, this type of applied research by religious scholars could be expanded to subjects like seminarians, priests, religious order members, and especially to the laity in numerous parishes and Catholic organizations. Rather than opinion from on high as to what people need, feel, or think, why not ask them through formal research, so as to adapt the planning and programs designed for their benefit? The implications are staggering for a metaindustrial, Information Society in which people seek more participation and involvement. Would that more Church "leaders" would follow the example set by this research effort. Social scientists engaged in doctoral research within Catholic universities are in a unique position to do this with their own religious systems.

Philip R. Harris, Ph.D., Management Psychologist and Author
La Jolla, California
(Former Catholic educational administrator)

INTRODUCTION

The Catholic church in the decades ahead will be shaped in considerable measure by its response *today* to the spiritual needs of the nation's Catholic youth. While the church should obviously not rush to adjust to every vagary of youthful opinion, it is important for church leaders to listen carefully to what youth today are saying about their faith if they hope to win or retain the enthusiastic support of these young people in the future.

To turn a deaf ear to the insistent questions of youth today — to ignore their pressing spiritual needs — to fail to give them that basic sense of self-worth that comes from knowing one is loved by God — is to store up serious problems for the church and for society as a whole in the years ahead. Low self-esteem, numerous studies have shown, is related to a host of social ills, including crime, school dropout and drug abuse.

Not only the church itself but society as a whole could be affected by the church's response to youth. Pope John Paul II in a March 26 letter to celebrate the 1985 U.N. International Youth Year urged the world's youth to "gradually succeed in changing the world, transforming it, making it more human, more fraternal — and at the same time more of God."

But how well are church leaders tuned in to the spiritual feelings of youth? And, are they making a real effort to understand young people who are only nominally Catholics and

2   Faith Without Form

perhaps outside the church entirely? Author Peter Feuer in the July 28, 1985 issue of OUR SUNDAY VISITOR writes:

"Rather than aiming to reach the large numbers of unconverted young people who hang out on street corners in virtually every city and town in the nation, the church has largely geared its youth programs to serve the many young Catholics who already come to our parishes of their own free will."

There is an urgency to finding out where young people are in their faith lives because the proportion of persons who describe themselves as Catholics tends to fall off rather markedly between the teens and adulthood — from 4 in 10 to 3 in 10 in recent years.

A 1985 survey for The Paulist National Evangelistic Association offers some key reasons why persons of all ages who once belonged to the Catholic church have rejected the idea of returning and, at the same time, important target areas for evangelistic efforts: unable to accept some of the Church's teachings (62% said this), factors related to priests (15%), the Catholic way of life is too demanding (14%), and the procedure of joining the church is too complicated (7%).

The question facing the church today is not only how well is it listening, but is it making full use of modern and reliable methods to enhance the listening process — namely, quantitative and qualitative survey research.

In their book *Faith Without Form* authors McAuley and Mathieson have done a masterful job of listening to the spiritual struggles of young people and their frustrations with certain aspects of organized religion.

They have given us solid statistics but have added life to the percentages with in-depth interviews. Indeed, one of the great strengths of their book, in my view, is the selection of revealing comments made by teenagers at all stages of faith development, giving us an excellent feel for the mood of Catholic youth today.

The authors point out that their book is not a guidebook, with a suggested list of "do's" and "don'ts". Yet in reading about youth attitudes on the family, sexuality, basic religious beliefs, organized religion, vocations, and other well-chosen topics, one comes away with definite ideas about what needs to be done. This quantitative/qualitative study is, therefore, highly actionable.

One message that comes through loud and clear is the need for a reassessment of religious education programs, in view of the serious lack of knowledge among young people about Christianity and the Catholic church.

The opening chapter also makes it clear that parents and teachers need to spend far more time in helping young people deal with the core questions in their lives — basic values, life goals and priorities.

There are many insights in this book — McAuley and Mathieson have listened well.

George Gallup, Jr.

1
THE STUDY

"You have great potential here with us if you only can be truthful. Most youth don't trust blindly and we don't trust what we don't know. We are neither children nor adults. We can be stubborn. We may seem to have no rules we abide by, but in general we do have some. We and our rules are the products of a turbulent era."

The Problems

This comment, verbatim, was written by a teenage girl, a practicing Catholic attending a coeducational Catholic high school, on a questionnaire asking students about their attittudes toward religion and the Catholic Church. It summarizes the problems facing anyone trying to answer the question: What do the Catholic teenagers of the 1980's feel about their church?

In a rapidly and radically changing world there is a perceptible revolution in values affecting the whole society, but that is particularly apparent in young people. It is inevitable that it should also become apparent in Catholic schools, which have been regarded for so long as very important guardians and nurturers of faith.

There has been much discussion and speculation during the past two decades over how young people relate to the post-Vatican II church. The general tone tended to be one of considerable pessimism, but this has sometimes seemed to be based more on perceptions than on hard data.

The Research

In 1983, the research reported in this book was undertaken to provide an in-depth examination of the perceived transition in belief, thinking and practices, as reflected in a random sample of the graduating classes of Catholic high schools in the Archdiocese of Washington, which includes suburban Maryland. The researchers considered insight into the feelings of these young people to be essential if educators, counselors, parents and other adult leaders are to establish lines of communication and provide effective guidance for the students' development. This view was shared by a number of bishops and others active in the field, and some of these were brought together to form the Advisory Board that guided the subsequent research. (Names of Board members as well as sources of funding are included in the Acknowledgements.)

The intention of this book is to provide a succinct account of the results of the research. It both reports on what the high school youth said on the questionnaires and in the course of personal interviews, and reflects on what their words imply. Both the reflections and the tentative recommendations developed from them come out of the authors' own experience and study, one as a member of a religious congregation which has played a key role in education, the other as a Catholic laywoman who has experienced her own struggles with the institutional church and can therefore empathize with the conflicts described by these young people, while at the same time realizing that there are no easy answers.

Certain major topics emerged from the study, and these receive special attention in the following pages. After a brief outline of the demographics of the participants, a separate chapter is devoted to each of these topics, which are: Values, clearly in a state of flux; Sex, which occupies much of these teenagers' attention; Prayer, which they feel is of great importance; Sin, which confuses them; the Church, which they see as a rather distant and strange entity; the Parish, which they know better and do not hesitate to criticize; and the Religious Life, which holds little appeal for them.

This research, carried out in the Archdiocese of Washington, D.C., included a random sample of 10 Catholic schools with a total of 784 high school seniors. They completed a six-page questionnaire designed to measure briefly their family background, religious beliefs, value systems, hopes for the future and the transformations taking place in their lives. The quesionnaire asked initially for demographic information, then obtained ratings for a number of social and religious values, and finally requested factual information about belief in God, religious practice and involvement in parish activities. The students were told that it was not a test, that honest answers were very important and that their anonymity was guaranteed. The study also captured the interest of the faculty in each school.

In addtion to the questionnaires, eighty in-depth interviews were conducted with a random sample of the surveyed population. Each interview lasted for approximately an hour and was taped with the student's approval. Topics covered in these interviews were divided into four major categories: general, beliefs/morality, personal transformation and stages of faith.

Student Reactions

Most of the participating students showed an unexpected eagerness to be heard. They displayed a marvelous openness, as will be obvious in the following pages.

There were a few dissenting voices, evidenced in answers to the final item on the questionnaire, which asked, "Are there any other comments you would like to make?" These seem to answer the cynics who question the authenticity of the responses, for example:

> I feel that there is no need to conduct such a survey because basically the ways people feel about religion and reality aren't compatible. All people are hypocrites in that they claim they accept their religious beliefs and follow the ways of their God, but reality shows us that these people are pulling the wool over no one's eyes except their own.

> I feel that all you people are poking into the young people's feelings. I question the "honest" methods you who call yourselves priests, nuns, brothers, sisters and ministers go about in surveying adolescents and the like.

> I hate the way these questions are subtly condescending.

> Some of these questions were none of your business because I really don't know if I should trust you. You can't just meet a person and trust them. You earn trust. Why is it that people are always trying to pester young adults about their religion? Why don't they just leave us alone? Maybe that's why kids turn away from the church. They're pushed so much that they get disgusted and don't care anymore.

However, the majority of the comments were positive, expressing in varying degrees the thoughts of one student who said:

> I think this survey was a very good idea. It helped us teenagers to be heard, for once. Usually no one wants to hear what you have to say.

2
THE STUDENTS AND THEIR FAMILIES

I do believe that over 50 percent of the kids today are out of touch with the church. I believe this may have something to do with how much trouble there is at home and if their parents have strong beliefs or not. Also, how open parents are about religion is important. I do not think religion should be forced upon a child or young adult. It pushes them further away. Values must be instituted at a very young age and have to also be consistent throughout our lives.

This student has gone to the heart of the matter. In spite of the considerable influence of religion teachers and parish priests, the atmosphere of the home, which is absorbed by children from their earliest years, lays the foundation of attitudes and values which may be adapted later but never completely erased.

The Students

Of the total number of students 433 (55 percent) were male and 342 (44 percent) female. (Percentages not totalling 100 indicate omissions by respondents and/or fractions of percentages.) The majority (81 percent) were 17 years old, with 7 percent younger and 11 percent older. Non-whites made up 45 percent of the total, whites 54 percent.

In rating their own academic standing, the majority (58 percent) said that they were in the middle of their class, 35 percent that they were near the top and seven percent that they were in the lower range.

Fifty-seven percent of the students said that their parents had the most influence on them, compared to 52 percent who cited their religion teachers. It became clear, however, particularly in the interviews, that many were not aware of how deeply their reactions to other questions were colored by their home background. An example of this is an apparently intelligent young man who spoke enthusiastically about the Church's teachings on love, only to say a few minutes later that, as far as he was concerned, the people of Asia could starve; and, while saying racial prejudice is stupid, he said he had never met a black person of any substantial intelligence. The tendency to accept parental opinions without a great deal of questioning was acknowledged by another male student:

> I guess I have been listening to my father and various older people, who when I was very young constantly railed against Vatican II.

The students reported that other influences on them — after parents and religion teachers — were less important, with Mass and religious services mentioned by 30 percent, priests by 19 percent and friends by 10 percent. Grandparents, TV/radio religious programs, newspapers and magazines all received less than 10 percent.

The Families

Thirty-three percent of the fathers were college-educated and

21 percent had postgraduate education, while 29 percent had high school educations, 7 percent had attended trade school, and 3 percent had only grade school education. Approximately 7 percent of the students did not know their father's educational level.

Thirty-nine percent of the mothers were college-educated and 12 percent had postgraduate education, while 35 percent had high school educations, 6 percent had attended trade school, and 2 percent had only grade school education. More than 4 percent of the students did not know their mother's educational level.

Seventy-three percent lived with both father and mother (in some cases this could mean a stepfather or stepmother), 20 percent with their mother, and 7 percent with either their father, grandparents, uncles and aunts or friends.

Fifty-one percent listed the occupation of the family's chief wage earner as business (office work, salesperson, etc.), 29 percent listed professions (teacher, lawyer, doctor, etc.), 9 percent listed day laborer and 9 percent listed "other."

Space was provided on the questionnaire for additional comments about themselves or their families, but few students took the opportunity. Only a minority spoke of the family as having had a positive influence on their religious life:

> My family is very religious. We go to church on Sunday and even holy days of obligation, so I've had a Catholic upbringing. Now I don't have to go to church but I do.

The interviews provided more comments on family situations, both positive and negative. One girl said that her parents mattered a great deal to her because with them she knows that she will always have someone to talk to, while a boy acknowledged this need but did not see it being filled by the family:

Everyone should have someone to talk to, because it's hard to talk to your family a lot of the time. The family might be close, but it's hard for the children to talk to the parents. A lot of the time the parents are the people who are putting the pressure on you.

Church Affiliation

Not all students in Catholic schools are themselves Catholics; 28 percent were not Catholic and no attempt was made to exclude the non-Catholics from the survey. However, as the major thrust of the study was to examine the perceived alienation of the Catholic teenagers (72 percent of the total) from their Church, the greater part of this book will be concerned with their comments.

Almost 59 percent of the fathers and 70 percent of the mothers were identified as Catholic, with 37 percent of the fathers and 30 percent of the mothers non-Catholic. Almost 2 percent of the students said that they did not know if they themselves were Catholic and 8 percent of those saying they were Catholic did not know if they were practicing their religion. Judging from their answers to the remainder of the questionnaire, this reflected the confusion that they were experiencing in trying to sort out their beliefs. Of the Catholic students, 75 percent described themselves as practicing.

Of the fathers identified as Catholic, 70 percent were described as practicing, as were 82 percent of the mothers; 3 percent of the students did not know their father's religion, but less than 1 percent did not know their mother's.

Almost 68 percent of the total (including non-Catholics) had attended Catholic grade school.

Several students said that, while their parents had forced them to attend church while they were children, they did not expect to continue once they left home:

> I go to Mass every Sunday. But the real reason I go is because my parents would get very upset if I didn't. It's alright sometimes, but most of the time it's boring. I'm afraid when I move out this summer I'm not going to attend Mass anymore, because there isn't going to be someone to tell me to go, and that worries me.
>
> Out of a family of five kids, I'm the only one who goes to church. I'm the only one left at home and all the others stopped going to church after they graduated from high school.

This raises a point that will recur frequently and be examined in more detail in the final chapter. Teenagers have an acute perception of parental fudging of values, which they identify uncompromisingly as hypocrisy. While they will usually go along with parental wishes while they are young and have no real choice, they are merely waiting to declare their independence from what they see as a phony religion.

Mixed Marriages and Divorce

There were many instances of "mixed marriages" and also of divorced parents in the families of the students surveyed. Where the parents were of different denominations, there could be evidence that the children had never developed a strong sense of belonging to a particular church, and they sometimes received conflicting messages from the two faiths. Divorce brought, along with all the inevitable pain and stress, situations where a child saw the Church as being indifferent or even hostile to a parent:

> Sometimes I have mixed feelings about the Church. My mother was divorced for very understandable reasons (the marriage has been annulled). She had

two children, no money and the Church (the parishes around this area) would not help her one bit.

At other times, the parent with whom the child spent weekends was a nonchurchgoer, and so the habit of Sunday Mass was broken.

Family Influence

There is another side to the picture, however, and not all students are in conflict with their families. One young woman said that she came to know God through her parents. Her mother was a convert, very religious, and so was her father. Her parents brought her up to be religious and taught her, even before she went to school, who God was and how to act.

The comments reflected the confusion that was apparent throughout the study, as these young people struggled to discover what, if any, relationship they could build with their Church:

> My family — especially my mother — is very concerned with religion. I have been too busy and too unconcerned to really stay involved with the Church, although I *do* want and need God's help in my life. My mom knows this and I think she worries about me. The thing is, although I realize this, I know I won't do anything about it.

Many of these students say that they expect to leave the Church when they move away from their family, even though God is important in their lives. Although the home influence is acknowledged, it may no longer be sufficient to keep them involved once they have gained their independence.

Even healthy families have to contend with the stress of a culture in which both parents frequently have jobs and therefore little time for active participation in parish and school activities. Many of the lay people do not understand, or keep current with, the changes in Church teaching and practice since Vatican Council II (1965). As a result, they may either cling to what they learned when they were young or have only a superficial, though well-meaning, understanding of current theology. In either instance, however sincere they may be, their practice is likely to confuse their children, especially when it conflicts with what they are being taught in school.

What can be done to strengthen the family influence when it is positive and to try to change it where it is destructive? Inevitably there will be many instances where nothing tangible can be done, and here the responsibility will fall more heavily on the school and parish.

Perhaps one of the best ways to help our children in their search for a Supreme Being may be to provide interesting, effective and substantive religious education for their parents. While this will not reach everyone, if it is done well it can produce results extending far beyond the actual participants.

Topics for Discussion

1. In what ways have the changes in the family affected the religious attitudes of children?

2. What can be done to help parents who want to transmit their faith to their children, but have difficulty combating a secular society?

3. What constitutes the Church's responsibility for the development of family life?

4. How much is rejecting organized religion a natural part of growing up, and what can parents do at this period to help ensure that the young person will eventually on his/her own, return to the Church?

5. How can adults relate to the concerns of teenagers, while still retaining and transmitting their own religious convictions?

3
VALUES AND PRIORITIES

> I believe that the church in general tries to make those who have a house, car, money and luxuries feel guilty about what they have bought with their hard-earned money. I've listened to many priests when they are giving the homily. They make me feel guilty that I go to the beach or ski or do anything that involves having more than someone else has. I know that there are poor among us. I know myself that I give food and money to the poor. Jesus said that the poor will always be with us. We should try to make their lives a little better. But when the priest makes those fortunate ones feel guilty because they have plenty, it makes me sick and it really turns me away from what they are saying. I'm not the only one who feels this way. A lot of people my age feel this way too. The way the church goes about it is wrong. They shouldn't have to lay a guilt trip on people to ask them to help the poor.

The students' responses to the acquisitive, consumer-oriented culture in which they are growing up ranged from the defensive tone of this quotation to unquestioning acceptance, to an attempt to develop different values. The defensive and accepting constituted the majority of the respondents.

Questionnaire Responses

To determine what their values were, students were asked to rank 17 items on a scale of one to five, with (one) rating low and (five) high. In order of perceived importance, these items were selected as follows:

Good physical health	92%*
A good family life	91%
An interesting and enjoyable job	91%
A good self-image	90%
Personal satisfaction or happiness	89%
A sense of accomplishment and lasting contribution	85%
An exciting and stimulating life	82%
Helping people in need	77%
Freedom to do what I want	76%
A high income	69%
Following God's will	68%
Many friends	64%
A nice home, car and other belongings	58%
Acceptance of peers	51%
A lot of leisure time	39%
Taking part in church-related activities	34%
Going to confession	22%

*Percentages indicate students selecting these items

Egocentrism

Teenagers are naturally self-centered; this is part of growing up. They are going through a difficult period in their lives, which can absorb most of their emotional as well as physical energies.

One male student summed up his own attitude in the following words:

> I want to make life as easy for myself as possible. . . .
> I try not to think about the future, I don't worry about the future very much. I think everything is one step forward, so I take life as it comes along.

Another said, "For myself, I just want a successful life, a good job." Yet there are signs of an awareness that the pervading materialism is potentially destructive:

> I think that because of my upbringing I have been trained to be too materialistic. This is a great concern of mine, and I don't find the words of God to be enough to help me. I think that it's a step in the right direction, however, when I can admit to myself that my priorities are wrong. I wish I understood why sometimes I feel very religious, then other times I don't. I wish I had someone to talk to that wasn't in some hokey church group.

A student at one of the city schools said that his dreams for the future included making a lot of money. However, he wanted to help his parents and also the poor overseas by sending them money. "I would feel," he said, "that God had given it to me and I should pass it on. If I can keep my faith up, my dream of helping can come true." He asked why we cannot use our abundance of food to help the needy. The same student wished that he could have seen Martin Luther King, Jr. in action, but said that among present day leaders he somewhat trusted Jesse Jackson and Billy Graham and would look for honesty and concern about people as important qualities.

Social Concerns

Students were also asked to give their opinions on seven statements dealing with social topics. Four of these were:

> Cheating in business is wrong.
>
> It's all right to get high on whisky or beer if you don't injure yourself or anyone else.
>
> It's all right to take hard drugs (cocaine, PCP, uppers and downers) to relax and have a little fun.
>
> Mercy killing for people suffering from a terminal illness should be allowed.

Cheating in Business

Eighty percent agreed that cheating in business was wrong, although the interviews produced an interesting rationalization of dishonesty:

> In business you can't be a total scoundrel, but if you don't cheat a bit you are going to sink. You'll probably put a couple of people on unemployment lines, not to mention yourself, so you have to do it to stay afloat. But you can do it — if there's such a thing — in a better way. You've got to compromise between the practical and the theological. I think it would be better for more people if I survived in business, so if I had to cheat I would do it. But I wouldn't be a J.R. Ewing, putting everybody down to be number one.

While this was the most outspoken comment, a number of

students felt that the Church had no business interfering in daily life and that it should tend to purely spiritual matters. In this they demonstrated only too clearly that they had missed the whole essence of Christianity — that it cannot be confined to one small segment of our lives, but must permeate and change everything that we do and are.

Politics and Justice

Two later questions asked whether the church should take public stands on important political issues such as the nuclear arms race, busing for school integration, equal rights, etc., or whether the church should take an active stand against such groups as the Nazi party, communists and the KKK, and the same questions were raised in the interviews. In response to the first question, 59 percent answered yes, 24 percent answered no, and 16 percent had no opinion. To the second question, 60 percent answered yes, 21 percent answered no, and 18 percent had no opinion. In response to a third question, 77 percent said that the church should give more financial assistance to the poor, while only 7 percent disagreed and 16 percent had no opinion.

Most of the students saw injustice as something unfair that had happened to them, such as bad treatment by priests, teachers or their peers. One exception was a white student at a suburban girls' school. She spoke of people's prejudice toward Jews and blacks, admitting that when she heard about the treatment of Jews in Nazi Germany she could not understand how a whole nation would follow a crazy man and persecute people just for their religion. She also expressed concern about Third World countries where everybody is poor except for those in the government and said that while she thought that Pope John Paul was trying very hard to set an example, she did not know if many people were listening to him.

Even when asked repeatedly about injustice in society, many

students had no reaction. Those who had ideas did not necessarily support the Church's position. Two young women reached similar conclusions from very different points of view:

> I think the Church puts too much of a guilt trip on people concerning justice, because you can only do so much. The Church should not get into political things or tell people what to do. The rich should help the poor but shouldn't be harped at about it. It turns me off when they harp on such problems.
>
> I feel that the Church attempts to give to the poor, but you have to realize that people also have to help themselves. As you get older, you have to realize that you've got to do something other than steal. You have to find a way, even if it is delivering newspapers, to support your family. Sitting back and collecting checks or being given a basket at Christmas, you can't just do that. If I was poor, I don't think I could have someone always supporting me. If I know that I'm old enough to support myself, I would do almost anything to take care of myself. I don't see putting the blame on the church, that it should help me more.

Some supported the concept of social justice but did not seem to want to get too close to the reality:

> I've worked on a project with the handicapped, but I feel that just because we don't go down there doesn't mean that we don't support it. There are some that are active and go down there, while some may support it with prayer, get funds for it. I think that we should help in some way, but we have to decide what is the best way according to our personality.

There were also rueful admissions of failure:

I think I could do more as far as helping out at the church, helping older people or people my own age. I think that's the way we were brought up, to help people but don't always expect something back.

One student saw the problems of Latin America as so complicated that there seemed little hope:

I thought that the pope's visit (to Central America) was trivial, because a lot of the guerrillas are Christian and are just looking for a better life, while the government, which is also Christian, sees the guerrillas as communists and anti-Christians. The pope was appealing to both sides, but neither side is really going to listen.

A male student at a suburban school became intemperate at what he saw as the Church's misguided involvement in the world:

I think for the church to get involved in politics is wrong. You read in the paper about Father So-and-so taking a stand and it just seems ridiculous, so out of place, making the church a joke because the church doesn't know. Flaming liberal priests just make the church look bad and I think they should keep a lid on them if people think they are a bunch of crazies. We go to church and that's one part of our lives, but to make it all of our lives is wrong.

Nuclear War

On the subject of nuclear war the prevailing reaction was one of concern and fear. One student confessed that the idea of nuclear war bothered him when he thought how someone could destroy thousands with the touch of a button for no good reason. He believed that the Church should take a stand because governments were not doing anything. A girl expressed very strong concerns about nuclear arms and the possible risks in having children under a nuclear threat. She said that she had been very frightened by a television program about nuclear terrorism. Another student commented fatalistically that he did not think there was much that one could do about nuclear war, because "the church can't stop the Russians."

Perception of Bishops

The only subject on which a number of students referred to the bishops was the letter on war and peace, *The Challenge of Peace: God's Promise and Our Response* (1983), in the news at the time. There was a tendency to assume that the bishops could not possibly be as qualified as these teenagers to speak on such worldly matters — perhaps not understanding that the destruction of the world was a matter of intense religious, theological and spiritual concern. Conceivably the students saw the bishops as somewhat remote individuals who appeared in the parish on rare ceremonial occasions, wearing strange vestments and quite without relevance to everyday life.

The following three quotations exemplify the students' reactions:

> Nuclear weapons concern us all, but the bishops are not looking at the facts. We are in the position where we have to keep it up just so we won't get into a nuclear war. They should understand that. They are not professionals and they have no right to be talking. It seems to me that we can't get into a war now because we can't fight one. The glory days are over. It's gotten a lot more complicated and you just can't fight anymore.

> I am against any type of nuclear freeze and I am angry that my Church supports this. Of all the anti-nuclear weapons groups that I have heard, both Christian and nonreligiously affiliated, all have been very biased. I would like to hear the arguments that our American bishops used in voting to ban nuclear weapons.
>
> I think it's good that the bishops want to have some influence; but it's not going to help much, because each government is set in its ways. I think that we should freeze no matter what. We already have enough to blow up the world, so what is the use of making more? Blow up the world a couple more times? One Trident submarine could disable the Soviet government, so what more could you need?

It might help to restore the balance if schools and parishes could devote some time to teaching about the role of the bishops in the modern world, with particular reference to those bishops whose pastoral concern and personal life-style make them admirable role models in a society that could use more examples of Christian living.

Technology

Not surprisingly, most of the students surveyed accepted the growth of the technology, but there was a different reaction from those from lower income families and those with affluent backgrounds. The former saw the threat to their own future as jobs were phased out with the introduction of computers and robots, while the latter concentrated on the advantages that they saw in these changes:

> I think the mechanical part of work is half of our human resources and if you chop that off, you are chopping off half of human nature. You are stifling

our growth. The people who now have jobs that can be done by robots are going to be in big trouble. Unless they can adapt to whatever they have to do and run the computer, they are probably going to be fired. We will probably have more of a recession and economic problems.

I think the computer is good as long as it's not misused. There is a lot of ignorance about computers and people fear them unnecessarily. The jobs people do will change around. It certainly won't hurt if people who are doing assembly line jobs don't have to do them any more. There will be other things they can do.

One student voiced an unorthodox opinion.

A friend who really knows the Bible says that computers are the work of the devil.

Drugs and Alcohol

When they spoke of drink and drugs the students were on more familiar ground. Fifty-five percent accepted getting high on alcohol, while only 10 percent approved of taking hard drugs. The following comment illustrates a misunderstanding concerning the risks involved:

I think some drugs are OK, but some are really horrible and I would never take them. Cocaine is a relatively safe drug compared to LSD, Speed, Angel Dust (PCP).

While most denied using drugs and claimed to drink moderately or not at all, they refused to judge their less restrained peers. Their attitude was that everyone must make an independent decision and that they had no right to criticize or question what others chose to do:

> I don't see anything wrong with drinking. If you are old enough to handle a gun, you should be able to handle beer. Unfortunately, there are problems and I think people should be educated how to handle it. Because you are not supposed to drink, everybody goes ahead and does it, particularly in my class. The idea is to drink as much as you can, because what else is there to do? A lot of people drink and I don't see why they should be stopped. Drink is an escape.
>
> I see a lot of people who use drugs casually and I don't think anything of it. It depends on how you look at it. I think marijuana is relatively harmless; you have to smoke a lot of it to get really out of control. It's like drinking too much and it's the same if you take too many drugs.

A young woman from a middle-class background disclosed her own experiences with drugs with surprising frankness:

> I used to smoke a lot of pot but now I don't smoke any. It puts me to sleep. It's a worthless thing for me. I know a lot of people who trip on acid. They don't do that a lot, but whenever they can. I tried that once and didn't like it. It was horrible. I found out afterwards about people having bad trips and that they set up trip tents outside concerts. I saw some of the people there who were freaking out and it was terrible. I would be so scared, because they say you see monsters coming at you, giant spiders, and I hate spiders. I saw someone inject heroin once and that was really disgusting. I hate needles.
>
> I know a lot of upper-class or middle-class kids sell

drugs, or you become friends with adults who are selling it. I used to do a lot of cocaine and had friends 45 years old that I would be hanging out with and I would buy coke from them. I have a girlfriend who sells it and she's 27. These people are not addicts. I've never met anyone who was dependent on coke, so I personally don't think it's an addictive drug.

I worked for the last two summers and I must have made $7,500. $4,000 went on coke. A gram of coke costs $100. When you first start out you usually need more, but when you start doing it more, it's easier. Only if you can afford a lot would you bring it out at a party. You would normally have four or five people at the very most, do a couple of lines. You can lick it and it numbs your mouth, which is a really neat feeling, like having a local anesthetic in your mouth but a little different. When you do it through your nose it numbs part of your face and you start moving faster. It's not like taking speed. Speed makes you really jittery. I would take speed sometimes and my legs would start to knock, but coke isn't like that; it's more relaxing but it gives you a lot of energy. How long it lasts depends on how good it is. I guess it would last about 45 minutes.

Teenagers seem to ignore warnings, threats and prohibitions when it comes to using drink and drugs — unless or until a tragedy brings the danger home to them.

Mercy Killing

The confidence in their own invulnerability probably accounted for the hesitation they showed when asked how they felt about mercy killing. None saw the question as applying to them, even at some time in the future, although they did occasionally relate it to the death of parents or grandparents. With no explanation of the term in the questionnaire it could be interpreted as either the right to refuse extraordinary measures involving life support systems to keep the heart beating in an otherwise moribund body, or euthanasia — the decision by others that a sick person is no longer of value to society and so may be killed. However, 34 percent of the questionnaire respondents said that they would allow the mercy killing of the terminally ill, although many specified that this should be the decision of the patient, not of doctors or family.

In the interviews it was explained that what was meant was euthanasia and it seemed that most students appreciated the serious implications, although one young woman said:

> You have to take each case differently. If an individual wishes to end his or her life because they feel they are ready, they should be allowed.

On the related subject of capital punishment, another student asked, "What gives you the right to kill somebody, even though they've killed somebody?"

Conclusion

The conflict between the traditional values of the family and Church and the contemporary values to which young people are constantly exposed by television, as well as by records, films and the materialistic world in which we all live, became very clear in this part of the study. Peer pressure is strong, even when there are loud claims of independence, because often this independence reflects a wish to share the values of the group rather than those of the family. The egocentrism of youth is reflected in comments like:

> I don't really care what others think of me. With the exception of my few close friends, the only other person who has to be pleased is me.

28 Faith Without Form

There is confusion, too:

> At this point in my life I am having great difficulty settling my opinions. I often do things that may be considered wrong religiously but that I find no harm or evil in doing. I have no set views and I am open to change.

Others showed frustration at the apparent ignorance and unconcern of others:

> I feel that Christians today are uninformed about the injustice and social sin that goes on from within the world.

The situation was summed up by the young man who said:

> A lot of people feel that they should be free to do whatever they want, that they shouldn't be told.

That may hold the key — when faced with rules, regulations and prohibitions the teenager is likely to take the forbidden road, simply to strike a blow for identity and independence. Once again, the power of example is much more effective and can remain as a source of stability and strength while permanent values are being developed.

Topics for Discussion

1. To what extent must the materialistic values of society be accepted as an inevitable part of life?

2. How can parents, teachers and others lead teenagers to a better understanding of values without alienating them further in the process?

3. How do we deal with the contradiction between the Church's

discouragement of accumulating wealth and power and the American society's encouragement of the same?

4. How can religion classes help teenagers to understand the values of the Church and embrace them as their own?

4
SEXUALITY, MARRIAGE AND DIVORCE

> How come the Church and others are always concerned with students' sexual behavior? They are going to do what they want anyway. So why worry about it? The more people talk about it, the more they do it. We feel pressure.

If the teenagers in this study had values that often differed from those of their parents or teachers, this conflict was most obvious in their attitudes toward sex. They might be unable to claim much experience in other matters, but in sex they felt that they really knew what they were talking about, at least as much as their parents and certainly more than the priests, brothers and sisters who were vowed to chastity and therefore could not be expected to understand the primacy of sex in their students' lives.

With few exceptions, the teenagers simply did not accept the teachings of the Church. Even those who agreed with the Church's point of view on all other matters had reservations when it came to sexuality, accepting premarital sex as a normal part of life.

Sex-related Questions

The three sex-oriented statements on which students were asked to express their opinions were: sexual relations before marriage are wrong; abortions are wrong; homosexuality is an acceptable life-style. Thirty percent agreed with the statement on homosexuality, but there was little comment. This either was not a subject that greatly interested them or they were not comfortable discussing it, although one young man who was interviewed said:

> Last year or the year before the Church said that it was OK to be homosexual as long as you don't commit any homosexual acts. This was an important step for society.

Premarital Sex

Even many of those who expressed complete acceptance of other aspects of the church's teachings were unwilling to agree that premarital sex should be condemned. Only 21 percent accepted the statement that sexual relations before marriage are wrong, and there was a perception that the church is preoccupied with condemning sex in all its manifestations while withholding compassion from those who are suffering for their mistakes:

> I think the church should stand by those young girls who get pregnant before they are married. I know some sisters (in convents) have set up homes for the girls, but I think the whole Church should stand by them.

One young woman, who claimed to be completely comfortable in the practice of her faith and with the beliefs of the church, at the same time stated that "there's nothing wrong with premarital sex." A number of comments by male and female students stressed the importance of caring for your partner rather than being promiscuous or seeking only a personal, physical satisfaction:

> Concerning premarital sex, I don't see why the church looks down on it. If you *really* love the girl I don't think it's wrong.

> I was taught not to accept sex before marriage. I think a lot of people think it is their right to do it whenever they want, because they enjoy it, but I think it is more of a privilege. You should be at least educated enough to know when it would be wrong. It's completely wrong if you are just trying to have a good time. That is a total misuse of sex. As long as you really care about the person, even if you don't have any intention of staying with them all your life, it is OK. That's what almost everyone I know feels.

The majority view was stated by the student who wrote:

> I believe that premarital sex is not wrong if you and your spouse (*sic*) are honestly in love.

One student argued that Adam and Eve were not married, while another made it an issue of mental health, saying: "I feel a sexual relationship is needed to be sane in our society." However, one young man commented that while his male friends tried to make a big thing of premarital sex, he had found that girls he had dated had not really been interested.

Both Catholic and non-Catholic students spoke of their conviction that the church is opposed to sexual relations of any kind, even in marriage, seeing it as a necessary evil for the conception of children:

> I think Catholics are too hard-nosed and stubborn about this subject. It's natural to have sexual desires, yet we are told to control them until we are married. That's too hard to ask people to do.

> I sometimes feel the church is a little behind on the times in areas such as premarital sex and divorce. I do realize the church must have standards for us to look up to.

Abortion and Birth Control

With premarital sex so widely accepted, it is not surprising that abortion was more familiar to these students than to earlier generations. While it may be surprising that almost half the students would accept abortion, at least on a limited basis and for grave reasons, such as a threat to the mother's life, a genetic disorder, or when the pregnancy results from rape or incest, many more shared the difficulty experienced by a large number of adults, including clergy and religious, in condemning all forms of artificial birth control. In fact, 67 percent said that it is possible to practice artificial birth control and still be a good Catholic. Some saw this as one good way of preventing the need for abortions. As one girl said:

> I think contraception is a good thing, to prevent pregnancy and avoid the need for abortion.

A common reaction was that as sex was natural it must be good:

> Contraception is very good. If God did not make sex to be enjoyed, he would not have given us the feelings — just the mechanics — and this way the risks of an unwanted baby are minimalized.

Two students spoke of *Humanae Vitae* (the encyclical "On Human Life" issued by Pope Paul VI in July, 1968, which resulted in widespread controversy) with rather different interpretations. One complained that "the question of contraception is pretty vague, especially as proclaimed in *Humanae Vitae*," while the other said that: "sexual relations before marriage are moral if both partners have been committed to each other. Contraception is also licit." This student then went on to say:

> *Humanae Vitae* and other similar articles are completely biased in that sex is viewed as evil, and Pope Paul probably detested sex for pleasure. Marriage is *not* for procreation, it is for both human beings to develop better.

In a society that encourages the idea that all wishes should be fulfilled immediately, whether for a new car, a new shampoo or a new lover, it is hard to convince young people that anything is gained by denying one of their most overwhelming desires, for sexual experience, particularly as this is not an artificial need manufactured by advertisers but one of humanity's strongest drives. This quotation is from a young woman:

> Teenagers have desires and want to experiment with sex. When I was young I thought you shouldn't have sex, but now I think you should. Not just go out and have sex with anybody, but if you have a special person I think they should experience it, because they have desires just like adults. They are taking on the responsibility of maybe having a child. They should be careful, but they have a lot of birth control methods out there, for the guys especially.

While 53 percent of the students said that abortion was wrong, many added comments saying that it was necessary to consider the individual situation:

> I feel that many people's opinions change after they are really in the situation. They may say abortion is wrong, but when they are pregnant they might change their minds.
>
> Abortions are right when the mother is in danger, financial instability, etc.
>
> Abortion is not bad unless it is done after the first two or three months of pregnancy, because before that the baby is not a real person. It can't feel and know all the things we do as grown people. Besides, if it comes into an unwanted world it will have a sad life.

One of the interviewees spoke with such stunning honesty of her own experience of both sex and abortion that she deserves to be quoted at length:

> I had sex before I realized what was involved and now when I look back I get angry at myself for doing that, because I worry that when I get married the first night's not going to be as special as it should be and what will my husband think of me. That's the only thing that worries me. I'm angry that I did lose my virginity. It happened when I was in eighth grade, five years ago. The boy was just a year older. It was just one of those things that happen. He was a virgin too. If you lose your virginity to some stud who thinks he's God's gift to the world, that's not as good, because he's not as careful with you.
>
> I haven't stopped having sex. I've been pregnant twice. I had an abortion, which I don't regret at all. The first was when I was in 10th grade, and then six months after the first one, which is really bad for your insides. I told my mother after the first one.

I lied to the clinic about when I got pregnant. It was a good clinic and they didn't say anything to me. I told them I was in my third month, so I think there was only a difference of two weeks. If you go into your fourth month they can't take you. I had problems getting the money together and (the father) was no help at all, so I went by myself. Since I couldn't get the money together, my girl friend lent me the money. I was miserable.

Afterwards, I got depressed because everywhere I went I would see babies, and everything on television seemed to be about babies and natural birth. I would start crying, because in a way I wanted to have it. Realistically I didn't think there was any way I could handle it. When I was a volunteer at the hospital I saw a 13 year old girl who was pregnant, and that takes guts. When I was depressed after the abortion I had lots of girl friends who had been through it.

I never told my mother about the second one, because that would have really destroyed her. It was easier. I didn't even tell the guy because I didn't want to go through what I had gone through before. I stopped seeing him for two or three months. I told him afterwards and he was shocked. He said he wouldn't have behaved (like the first boy). He didn't think I should have had the baby, but he was wondering what it would have looked like.

I want to have kids, but it looks like it hurts an awful lot, so I think I would rather adopt.

Marriage

There was no separate item in the questionnaire asking students if they hoped to marry, but many brought up the subject in their answers to the question on vocations. Of those saying that they were not interested in the religious life, 23 percent wanted to marry and/or have children, while another 3 percent believed they would have problems with celibacy. It is reasonable to assume that many others also planned to marry but did not mention this.

During the years since Vatican II there has been a new emphasis in the church's teaching on marriage. The parents of today's young adults grew up in a time when marriage was primarily a social event. Preliminaries focused on making sure that there were no religious obstacles — the once familiar Sunday announcement during the "reading of the banns" that "if any of you know of any impediment, either of consanguinity, affinity or spiritual relationship," they should tell their pastor forthwith. Pregnant young women were hurried to the altar as quickly as possible, without questions being asked about the health of such a hasty marriage between two people who had just demonstrated that they did not look ahead to the consequences of their actions.

Today there is much more pre-marriage involvement on the part of the Church, with many dioceses setting a waiting period of six months or more before the ceremony can take place. During this time the couple is required to attend classes or discussions to make sure that they understand they are entering into a sacrament, with all the lifelong implications that this carries with it.

Many parishes have not explained this new emphasis and, of course, those who rarely go to church can hardly know about it. As a result, engaged couples and their parents sometimes receive an unpleasant surprise when they go to the rectory to make the wedding arrangements, and may attack the Church for what they see as unreasonable demands:

> In my opinion the Catholic Church is making it harder for people to return to the Church. There are too

many rules. For example, my brother wanted to be married in a certain Catholic Church, but because he did not practice his religion and was not a member of that parish, the priest told him that he could not be married there. He then found a church (where he could be married), but it made him angry, because he was making an attempt to help his faith and was refused. Also, there were classes on finance and other matters that he and his fiancee had to take which were not at all useful or helpful to them.

There was some discussion of marriage and divorce in the interviews. The notion that a couple could live together for a time in order to discover whether their marriage would work was raised. One male said:

> I think people have a misconception of what marriage is supposed to be. There are so many people I know in this school whose families have been divorced. It's really amazing. I come from a family where no one has even thought of it. I could see living together as a pretty good way of getting to know a person, and then have a really healthy marriage built on respect.

A young woman, a non-Catholic, said:

> A lot of kids say that sex should be right before marriage, because you can always love somebody before you get married. If you really love and care for each other, if you get married the time period shouldn't make a difference. Marriage is a big thing and you'll be spending the rest of your life with that person.

The bad results that can come from parental pressures and family conflicts were also mentioned:

> I had a friend who got married really early because her parents told her that they wouldn't approve of it. She did it just to prove to them that it would work and it didn't.

Another student related the problems of marriage to the increased life expectancy, which prolongs the length of marriage far beyond what it once was:

> Teenage marriages scare me. If you get married at 17 you'll be with that person for the rest of your life. In the 17th and 18th centuries, life expectancy was short but now it's much longer.

Divorce

It was, therefore, natural that the students should also wish to talk about the Church's attitude toward divorce, which they often misunderstood. This should not be surprising, as it is obvious to anyone who reads the letters to the editor in a typical Catholic diocesan newspaper that the subject also confuses priests, teachers and other adults.

One of the points of misunderstanding was the belief that divorce itself, rather than remarriage after divorce, separates one from the reception of the sacraments or even ends membership in the church. However, two percent of the respondents stated that a divorced person should not be allowed to receive communion, an example of students stricter than the Church.

Another problem area involved remarriage. Some of these students spoke from experiences in their own families when they championed the right to remarry:

> One of my big problems with the Catholic church is their opinion of divorce. I'm not saying that it is right, because I think it is wrong; but it has affected me

personally. My father was married and divorced before he met my mother. Now she can't go to communion at Mass every Sunday. It burns me up to see her just sit there every week.

There was also a sense of injustice if people continue to be punished for their mistakes — something that seemed at odds with the idea of a loving and compassionate God:

> I think the Church is being a little too stubborn on divorce. The divorce rate has shot up and some of it is because people are getting married for the wrong reasons, but some of it is because they can't stay together without fighting and then it is better to get divorced. I think they should be able to get married again. It didn't work the first time, but perhaps it will go right the second time. I don't think it's right for them to live their whole life alone. I don't think they should get remarried the day the divorce papers come through, but if they really find somebody that they love, then I think it would be all right to get remarried.

> I don't believe in divorce, but in the case of a battered wife or an alcoholic wife or husband it's hard. I guess that there should be a counseling period. If a divorced person wants to remarry, that shows that there has to be something good about marriage. I don't think they should remarry right away, because that's not saying much about their conception about marriage.

Others overlooked the commitment required in marriage and equated it with romantic love:

> I think the church should stand by those who wish to get a divorce. It is better to leave your wife/husband if you no longer love the person than to stay

there and pretend that you do love them.

If divorce and remarriage caused confusion, this was mild when compared to the passionate attack launched by one student on the annulment of marriages by the church.

> I think people should not and the Church should not make accommodations for social wrongs just because times have changed. An example . . . is the annulment of marriages by the Church. The Church by this action professes a marriage to be null and void. This means the marriage never existed, which is wrong. If a marriage has lasted for 25 years and children were reared, this means the children are illegitimate, which is not true. These children now bear the social name of bastards, which they are not. When I think of such actions . . . I wonder what is next.

As more and more marriages are annulled in the United States, this is surely another area that calls for clear and compassionate education, in the schools and from the pulpit, so that unnecessary suffering and guilt can be avoided.

Conclusion

The difficulties and disagreements described in this chapter may perhaps be explained by considering the gap that often exists between the current teachings of the church and the actual teaching by the church's representatives in parishes and schools. The differences that occur are illustrated by two examples. The first student said:

> Last year we discussed sex and were told that petting is bad. I think that some parts of it are bad, but they said that kissing was bad and I disagree with that.

> I don't see exactly how that's immoral. They seem to be a little rigid on that matter. I don't think premarital sex is right, but I don't think that the church's teaching on sex speaks to my generation. Pope John probably updated it, but I think it's got to be updated again. Vatican II ended in the 1960s, so that is one or two generations before our time. I think it has to be looked at again, because people change.

The second student told the interviewer that they were taught that in each of us there is a part of God. Sex shouldn't be abused just for pleasure, because it is the greatest way to express love for another person, and she added: "How can you know if you love that person unless you make the greatest commitment, which is marriage?" More teaching which accepts the reality of the sexual urges but also stresses the importance of personal values, might avoid at least some of the problems that teenagers experience.

Students seem to have not always listened to what the Church is saying, as when one complained:

> I think more churches should take more time on talking about specific topics such as abortion and the pro-life movements. These groups of people need others who are willing to help.

Even a superficial reading of Catholic periodicals would show that this is not a neglected topic and the explanation may be that students are obtaining all their information in school or church and doing little reading, beyond what is required in their religion classes. As quoted in *Our Sunday Visitor* (July 21, 1985, p. 3), "The textbooks used in sexuality classes in Catholic schools have to be so safe that they say nothing."

The confusion and involvement shown on this subject is not

limited to youth and any study of adult Catholics would produce similar responses. While these students reflect the ideas of many of their elders, they also often have an incomplete understanding of what is actually said in Church documents such as *Humanae Vitae,* and they feel irritation at what they see as a complete lack of awareness of the real world of sexuality exemplified in the words of a celibate hierarchy.

Teenagers, who sometimes seem to treat sex as their preferred extracurricular activity, tend to blot out anything that the Church says on the subject, particularly when the teachings are presented by celibates whom many view as oddities with no idea of what life is really like.

Since 1969, the percentage of Catholics disapproving of premarital sex has fallen from 72 percent to 33 percent based on a 1985 OSV/Gallup poll. As pointed out in the article of *Our Sunday Visitor* previously mentioned, "Premarital sex is a tough problem the Church must solve." It may be that the only people with any chance of providing a healthy understanding of sex, of its emotional and spiritual as well as its physical dimensions, are those who are married — and not only married, but also happy and confident in their own sexuality and able to speak openly about it. There have been too few such people involved with teenagers in the past. It is imperative that more be encouraged to share their wisdom in the future.

TOPICS FOR DISCUSSION

1. To what extent is it realistic to expect teenagers to refrain from sexual intercourse in a society that takes it for granted?

2. How can parents and teachers instill an understanding of the beauty of sex in a way that is acceptable and realistic?

3. To what extent must parents and teachers alter their own life-style to meet what they are teaching young people?

4. How can parents, without sounding preachy or "know-it-all",

help young people understand that sexual relations at their age is more than a clear cut issue of right or wrong, that emotionally there is much at risk for them without sounding preachy or "know-it-all"?

5. Who or what really influences students when they make decisions on sex (family, religion, personal morals, peers, media etc.)?

5
GOD AND PRAYER

> You are leaving the God age and turning more to the machine age, and that's a little hard.

The research that forms the basis for this book did not attempt a detailed investigation of the students' perception of God, but did confirm the importance of the influence of families on children's religious faith, with 57 percent saying that religion was fairly important in their family, 35 percent that it was very important and only 8 percent that it was not at all important.

Concepts of God

It also produced a higher percentage of students who said that they believed in God — 92 percent, while 95 percent said that they prayed (one can only assume that the additional 3 percent were hedging their bets here). One student explained:

> Religion was never very important to me, but recently I've been changed in that attitude. Now it is the greatest influence on me. I don't think about religion and God all the time, but I do find myself turning and thanking God for something good and

asking him for help or the right thing to do. I wish that there was more of a way to show others just how important God is.

Sixty eight percent believed that God observes their actions and rewards or punishes them (one said that "God looks over my shoulder a lot."); 65 percent believed that God has a plan for their life; and 70 percent believed in a life after death. From the evidence of the interviews, students seemed to find it difficult to describe their perception of God, although several said that they no longer had their childish idea of God as an old man with a white beard. Sometimes they quoted the formula they had been taught:

> God is the Supreme Being who created everyone, for us to serve him and for him to love us.

Some had experienced the absence of God or found it hard to believe in his loving presence when they saw suffering or injustice:

> I do believe in God, but at times I wonder just where he is or why he lets some things happen.
>
> At this point I'm not sure what I feel. There is so much pain and suffering in this world that it is hard for me to believe in God. If he is so good and loves us so much, why do we go through this pain? Are we paying for something that we had nothing to do with or are we really in hell? It seems to me, with the suffering on earth, if this isn't hell, it can't be much worse.

The idea of growth through suffering does not appeal to a society convinced that it is entitled to a rose garden and inclined to believe that when the Declaration of Independence spoke of happiness, it intended that happiness be possessed by everyone as a right, rather than merely pursued.

Two reactions occur to one. The first is to regret that no one seems to have successfully explained to the students that there are difficulties inherent in these questions and that they need to understand at least the existence of the attempts to wrestle with them. Secondly, one can be grateful that they are aware of the problems, that they are questioning and searching, and trust that God will lead them, in his own good time, to a deeper understanding and faith. It is the old struggle between the idea of "blind faith," accepting the teaching of the church without question, and the encouragement of an informed faith, with all the risks that go along with this. On the evidence of these responses, the church at present is failing on both counts, unable to demand unquestioning obedience and not marshalling either the arguments or the examples to convince.

One student represented a fairly common attitude when she confessed that she considered God important in a crisis, as when her grandfather was in the hospital, but that otherwise she was not too aware of him.

Others were struggling to discover just what they believed in:

> I think questions should be asked about why people believe in God, because I know that it is always getting harder for me to believe.
>
> At my stage of life I'm somewhat confused about what I believe, because sin is a part of everyday life.
>
> There is so much that needs to be answered. Lately I have been going to different churches, talking to different people about this. There are so many religions with so many different beliefs, who knows what to believe? I just believe in God and that he will lead the way for me.

Many had obviously thought a great deal about God and their relationship with him. One student found that God gave meaning to his life and that it was a comfort to know he is there, while another defined God as "happiness, love." Others shared the feelings of the student who said:

> I talk to God friend-to-friend. I don't get down on my knees and think of him as way out there. I guess I don't have reverence for him, but think of him as a friend.

This idea of God as a friend who is always available is an important one and occurred again and again:

> God makes a difference in certain ways, like when I go through problems and stuff. I don't just call on him when I'm down and need help. I call on him all the time. I pray to him every night and when I wake up. In a way he's more than a friend. Even though I can't see him physically, I relate to him mentally.

> I have my own idea about God and religion and I feel God and I have an understanding. I pray a lot and we talk (or I talk). I work things out and believe what I want to believe and I feel this is right.

A natural consequence of the idea of God as primarily a personal friend is a reduction in the importance of community worship in a formal setting:

> I feel personally that you don't always have to go to church to talk to God, so sometimes I don't go to Mass on Sundays, but always, every day, I talk to God two or three times. When you are at church you are not really alone talking with God, it's more a community-type thing. I like the more personal con-

versations. Sometimes I have a guilt feeling but I realize that God understands that people have different schedules. I am a very busy person. I do believe that you should take time out for God, because he did create you and gave you life. So I do feel guilt sometimes, but not all the time. I know I have other things that he knows should be done.

The majority seemed to see their relationship with God as a very personal matter, and one in which they should be free to determine the structure.

I wish I could be more in tune with God. I don't like going to church; it does nothing for me. I would like to develop my personal religion much more. It seems that other things in my life override and block out religion.

I believe that I can be a good Christian without going to church or going whenever I want, when my faith is being tested. I also believe that I can talk to God any time I want when I pray and I don't have to go to a priest. If God made us and knows us, he can forgive us! That's what I believe.

When the students spoke of God it seemed that they were almost always referring to the first person of the Trinity, God the Father. A few spoke of Jesus in explaining why they preferred the New to the Old Testament and said that they "tried to do what Jesus taught." They tended toward an oversimplified concept of God, as someone or something that is "out there" to be talked to, to be asked for comfort and support, but with little more depth or complexity than this. There is hardly any suggestion of the infinite mystery of faith or awareness that there are depths of spirituality that may require a lifetime to explore.

> I believe in God, he's helped me so much. I do things wrong and I know it, but he never leaves me. I'm ashamed of myself and I really mean it.
>
> I feel that I have a deep faith. Even though I don't go to church except on holy days of obligation, I believe in God very strongly and try to uphold his commandments.
>
> There is some supreme force that unites our world together. "God" is not some old man who doles out forgiveness. God is the goodness we find in ourselves.

Other students had trouble in dealing with symbols and asked for "proof" of something more concrete:

> I believe in God most of the time, but I have my doubts a lot. I don't have my doubts in him when I don't get something I wanted, but when I see that just everything is a symbol. It seems that everything in our religion was just made up. There are no facts.
>
> My religious beliefs are mainly based on my ethics of right and wrong and not so much on what I have been taught. As with many things, it's hard to believe everything you hear with no real sound proof. But I do believe something or someone has to control the many things that happen and therefore I strongly believe in God.

Freedom of choice includes the freedom to decide not to believe, as two students made obvious, although with rather muddled logic:

> I *might* 'acknowledge' God's existence but I don't worship him. Did you ever think you might be worshipping two gods, by believing in and avoiding Satan —

as well as fearing him you are worshipping him. I don't believe in Satan. Man created God.

I don't believe in a God who has created the world and the humans who live there. I believe in a more scientific approach, such as evolution. I believe that there are higher forms of intelligent life (as well as lower) but not one creator of the universe. God seems to be something made up by man to explain ideas which are inexplicable. Religion therefore shows man's ignorance of true creation.

Prayer

Ninety-five percent of the students said they prayed, 48 percent at least once a day. However, only 52 percent said that they attended religious services weekly, with another 18 percent going once or twice a month. The students were also asked whether they read the Bible. Fifty-six percent said that they did not, while the interviews suggested that many of the 43 percent who said they did limited such reading to religion classes. Several comments echoed the student who said:

> The Bible is outdated. It doesn't keep up with the times.

Another remarked that, while he could not accept a great deal of the Old Testament, the New Testament meant a lot to him, because:

> It's not the parting of the Red Sea thing. It's actual, the guy's here, the real man, the real flesh. He's poor and he's disliked by many, but he's peaceful. The New Testament has a lot you can learn.

There were also those who were confused by the more complicated concepts that they were faced with in high school, and by what they saw as the personal interpretation of their teachers:

> During my years in school from first to eighth grade I was taught the basis for the Bible. The answers on tests were just fact. In high school I studied the Bible more in depth. A lot of the answers were opinion-based, but the teacher graded by his or her opinion only. It really messed my head up about religion.

One of the interviewers summarized her impressions by saying that the students had spoken of prayers of thankfulness, prayers to achieve an objective or personal request, and prayers of appreciation, most of these being informal conversations with God.

There was little mention of formal prayer. A typical response was:

> I don't read the Bible but I do pray. I think prayer is reflection — what have I done and what do I have to do? If you take the time you can really improve yourself and that's what I figure life's all about, making the best of yourself. When you just ramble off the Our Father and the Hail Mary, sometimes you're tired and you don't even know what you're saying. If you asked people to say them slowly they probably couldn't even do it. I think those prayers, when they're said that way, you're not even thinking about it.

While 6 percent said that they belonged to a prayer group, 93 percent stated that they would not be interested in joining one. An alternative to prayer was to substitute social justice activities, as if this were an either/or proposition: "Religion to me is helping the poor, rallying against handguns and lobbying for human rights, not going to church and praying."

An interesting point is that nowhere in this study did any student mention a single saint. Admittedly, no questions specifically addressed this subject, but the fact that no one brought it up, even in the course of extensive comments and interviews, suggests that saints play little or no part in their lives. The role models that Mary and the saints offer would seem to be lost to them.

Conclusion

One result of the vague approach to prayer evidenced in the study is that there is nothing specifically Catholic or even Christian in it. Such prayers could be addressed to the Buddha, to the Great Spirit of the American Indians or to any number of other concepts of the deity. This is not to denigrate these non-Christian religions, but to ask how these graduates of Catholic high schools will be able to remain faithful to a religion which they see as so formless, with so little definition, without a clear, valuable and attractive identity to which they can relate.

In short, the survey leaves us with an impression of high school seniors who believe in a God of whom they have a rather confused impression, who pray but mainly in an unfocused and private fashion, without much knowledge or appreciation of the riches available in the formal prayers of the Church, who demand to make their own decisions about their religion but seem not to know that there are road maps, guidebooks and memoirs of those who have already made the same journey to which they could turn for enlightenment.

Topics for Discussion

1. How important is it that Catholic high school students learn the doctrine of the Catholic Church?

54 Faith Without Form

2. Is it sufficient for students to believe in a personal God and to pray in an unstructured fashion?

3. What can be done to help young people have a better understanding of what God can mean in their lives?

4. How can the Church help students to be aware of the different forms of prayer?

6
SIN

I don't believe in sin. I think that mistakes are human and if Jesus was human he must have made some too!

The Meaning of Sin

The presence of sin and evil in the world may be one of the most difficult problems that anyone can confront. Through the centuries and at all levels of theological sophistication it has been discussed and debated. It is, therefore, not surprising that this should be a subject on which the students in this study showed the most confusion and the least understanding of the traditional and current teachings of the Church. If one has only a hazy idea of God, it follows that one is also likely to have a hazy idea of sin. The students' tendency to see God as a friendly "something" out there, asking only that they should be well intentioned, led them to assume that they could define sin according to their own desires and convenience. It seems that they had not read or thought about Webster's definition of sin as a "voluntary transgression of religious law or moral principle." Instead, we have statements like the following:

> Basically, if you have thought about what you are doing and whether for you it is right or wrong, it

really wouldn't cross my mind that it would be a sin. It would be just a normal everyday thing.

In 1973, Karl Menninger wrote a book that went to the heart of this problem, *Whatever Became of Sin?* These students seemed to have failed to understand the distinction between good and evil, right and wrong. Many appeared to have accepted the attitudes of a society where the refusal to take responsibility for one's actions and an emphasis on self-interest are commonplace. Forty-five percent indicated they had sometimes done something seriously wrong, 14 percent often, 37 percent rarely, and 3 percent never. While 62 percent indicated that their idea of sin had changed in the last four years, 37 percent gave a negative response.

Presumably, their home training and religion classes had not convinced them that there are such things as divine laws and moral principles, which are not subject to adjustment to meet one's personal wishes — or perhaps they had failed to understand these ideas. This could partially result from some of the texts being used in the schools, which tend to avoid clear definitions, preferring to approach the subject of sin on a very personal level, stressing the fact that one's conscience provides the norm for morality and seeing laws as merely guidelines to aid in the control of external actions in order to preserve inner freedom. Nothing there suggests that one's own definition of what is needed to enhance "inner freedom" may not only be contrary to the definitions of one's neighbors, but may also be in direct opposition to those divine laws and moral principles.

This is demonstrated in the comments of a student from a suburban highly academic school:

> The way I see it is that if you think something that the Church says is wrong for you and you are willing to stand up and accept the punishment, if you realize that this might hurt you in your afterlife, you should

go ahead and do it. I don't think you should just cower back because of what somebody else says. A lot of people aren't standing up for their own beliefs, but they don't agree with what the Church says, so they are just going to ignore it. They aren't taking into account that what they are doing is wrong and they are going to have to pay for it later. They just say, "I don't like it, I'm not going to do it." They just wipe it off their rule book.

Milton's Lucifer would have recognized a kindred spirit!

Rather than debate the relative merits of various texts on the subject, it is probably wiser to turn to what the documents of Vatican II have to say about sin. From these documents, which can be accepted as the authoritative voice of the Church in the latter half of the 20th century, it is possible to extract five brief statements to provide the foundation for an informed understanding of sin.

1) Personified evil seeks to turn humanity against God. This results in the loss of harmony "with himself, with others, and with all created things."

2) Life is a continual struggle between good and evil.

3) There is a law, beyond the individual, to which we owe obedience, and which manifests itself through our conscience.

4) Conscience can err due to ignorance or habitual sin.

5) The good news of Christ combats and removes these evils and errors. We cannot overcome sin without the intervention of Christ and the love that he has shown us, culminating in his death and resurrection.

The Results of Confusion

The absence of a clear understanding of these fundamental concepts seems to have resulted in much of the confusion and even error apparent in the responses of the students.

School texts, while for the most part technically correct, are often less than crystal clear and open to a very wide range of individual interpretations, particularly by young adults who are at an age when they naturally question what they are told and prefer their own interpretation. What seems to be missing is the awareness that the intrinsic sinfulness of an act does not depend on the casual decision that "I think that this is right for me." Although the subject is difficult, the responses suggest that the pendulum may have swung too far from the days when obsessive concern with humanity's sinfulness led to a preoccupation with heavenly bookkeeping and the rating of every action as more or less sinful.

It is extremely difficult to categorize the responses to the question, "Has your idea of sin changed in the last four years?" A large number of students seemed to have great difficulty putting their ideas into words, and it is impossible to guess what may have been meant by responses like:

> Because I learned that if you keep it up why bother to continue to do it?

or

> In what constitutes sin?

Very few appeared to hold the clear-cut, black-and-white, fundamentalist concept of sin demonstrated by one response: "Sin is not obeying every sentence in the Bible word per word," which might prove difficult to put into actual practice! It is clear, however, that many students were having trouble as they struggled to arrive at a more mature understanding of sinfulness. It is no criticism to say that they were finding it hard — it is as hard as anything they will have to do in their lives. What does give cause for concern is that a number of them seem to be out in the open sea in small boats without oars or compass and heading for strange and probably unintended destinations.

Increased Lenience

The largest number (24 percent) said that they now take a more lenient view of their actions, sometimes as a result of being less active in the Church.

> I have learned more things that do not hurt anyone are not sins, as before I believed they were.

> God was more a part of my life then than now. Without that discipline I've kind of done my own thing . . . and I'm not as conscious about my sins. I guess I've become more liberal.

Some were specific about the actions that they do not consider to be sinful:

> I don't feel that stealing is always a sin.

> I don't feel it is sinful to become drunk. I don't feel it is sinful to have a serious relationship (excluding intercourse).

> I feel as though an abortion is permissible in cases of incest or rape.

> I thought that just telling lies (like white lies) were sinning, but I don't think so any more.

> I don't think that missing church or not believing in God is a sin any more.

Premarital sex was specifically mentioned 17 times, in such comments as:

> I at one time thought sex before marriage was wrong. But it is a physical way of showing your love for each other.
>
> I used to think divorce and premarital sex were mortal sins, but I no longer have that feeling.
>
> I don't believe premarital sex is sinful.

The majority made more general statements, saying that they have become more "lenient," or "liberal," or "open minded." They were indifferent about actions that a few years ago they regarded as sinful. "My conscience is not bothered by minor things as much." There was less feeling of guilt. Earlier beliefs were seen as superstitions or myths. One student commented: "Things aren't as bad as people say." There was a general acceptance of the idea that "everything the Church thinks is wrong isn't always wrong." With this questioning of authority went a general loosening of earlier restraints and a willingness to make their own decisions, "for better or worse, I can't say yet." They had come a long way from the days when "a sin was something that you did which displeased your parents. It was called a sin and you could go to hell." That such independence is not all gain is illustrated by statements such as this: "Now I do a lot of bad things which would be considered sinning, but it doesn't bother me as much."

Another 21 percent said that they had learned more about sin during the previous four years, but did not always indicate what form this learning had taken. Their comments included: "I can't judge someone else's morality"; "I look more on what sin does to others"; "I have a clearer understanding of what is right and what is wrong"; "I have come to find out that sin is a very serious thing"; "There are many more factors involved in committing a sin than I had realized"; "I realized that it is possible to sin by thinking"; "I have matured in many ways. I learned the virtues and values of life, in being a Christian"; "I feel I'm more responsible for my actions."

Troubling Questions

If we take the optimistic view that these students have indeed learned but have simply failed to spell out their experience clearly, there may be little to worry about. As always, however, it is the responses of those who were more specific that tend to catch the eye and raise troubling questions.

Some 8 percent had taken the idea of the individual conscience and interpreted this as meaning that each individual is free to develop his or her own definition of sin, without reference to any outside authority. Their statements played variations on the theme "I have to do what I think is best for me, even if it does not fully agree with the Church." The key words here are "best for *me*," and they open up a limitless vista of self-interest, in their disregard for the well-being of others as well as of any divine laws. Other similar comments included:

> What's bad to you might not be to me.
>
> The Church's idea of sin and my idea of sin is entirely different. Since I am getting older, I am learning and making mistakes without the church telling me what's right and wrong.
>
> Sin is not cut and dried. It is a personal thing, which only the individual can judge. A certain act or lifestyle may be morally wrong to a particular group of people, but perfectly moral to others.

The origin of such comments may be found in some of the responses which speak of how the students were taught in grade school and even in the lower grades of high school. Those students who had been threatened, literally, with hellfire for childhood misdemeanors seemed to have more trouble in developing a mature concept of sin and to be more likely to toss out the whole idea and operate on the belief that sin depended on their own wishes. While this could reflect a better understanding of personal responsibility, it could also lead to the conviction that anything goes, provided that it meets one's own needs or desires. It is sad to believe, as one student wrote, "When you are little you feel that everything you do is wrong." The temporary obedience to authority that this may have produced in children may well be paid for later by their rejection of all belief in sinfulness, when they interpreted their teachers as grossly exaggerating the gravity of their misdeeds or mistakes.

> In grade school everything was a sin. Now I don't consider many things people do sinful.
>
> I no longer feel that little trivial things that happen in everyday life is a sin. Before, I was so paranoid that everything I did was a sin. I began to realize that not everything I did was wrong, i.e., I used to believe (when I was little) that if I ate a cookie before dinner, when my mother told me no, that I would be condemned for life.
>
> I thought every little thing I did wrong was a big sin and God would take it out on the ones I love.
>
> I don't think having a good time, partying occasionally, is a sin. I've been taught that it is a sin. I feel that as long as I am able to separate the good times from serious times (school, work, etc.) then it's OK.
>
> At my grade school they really scared you about sinning. Everything you did was practically a sin. They

really went by the old ways. If you wore your top
button undone you were sinning. I understand better
and if I'm sorry God will forgive me.

As they moved through high school and were exposed to a more subtle and nuanced theology, many apparently became confused. Once the idea took root that sin is not always a question of black and white, many rushed to the conclusion that anything that they enjoyed doing is not sinful.

Offense Against God and Others

There were two other groups — those who believed that sin is primarily an offense against God (3 percent) and those who believed that it is an offense against other people or against oneself (also 3 percent). The first group tended to be among the most articulate and to have the best understanding of the subject:

I believe sin is rebellion against God. I believe it is
not going God's way in order to go your own way. I
used to think that sin was breaking do's and don'ts.

Sin involves a little more than just being hardheaded.
You must turn your back on God and your fellow
man for it to be a real sin.

I believed that sin was doing anything that the
Church said was wrong. Now I believe that sin is
anything that alienates you from God or from your
neighbor.

An additional 4 percent of the respondents spoke of their need for God's forgiveness and their understanding of what this forgiveness involves:

> I believe God forgives us *only* if we are *sincerely* sorry. I used to believe God forgave everything.
>
> Four years ago I would have thought that if I sinned against God he would get me back for it.
>
> God is not just waiting to punish you for a sin; in fact, he is more willing to help and forgive than to punish.
>
> God wouldn't punish you for doing what you honestly thought was right.
>
> Before, I thought sins were unforgivable. Now, however, I know that through repenting a person can be forgiven all his or her sins.
>
> God will always give a person a chance to be good and will look at them individually to see their circumstances.

The understanding of those who said that sin was an offense against others or themselves tended to omit references to God and suggested instead various forms of humanism. Typical comments included:

> It's causing harm to yourself or someone else.
>
> Building weapons to kill is a sin. Hurting others is more serious than doing something wrong such as cursing, pornographic things, premarital sex, etc.
>
> I think that one sins when one goes against his/her moral standards.
>
> Sin to me is not eternal damnation, it is a resistance against one's individual beliefs and ideas. 'Sins' are not committed against someone — they are committed against yourself.
>
> Sin is hurting others. What you do to yourself is your own problem.

Strict Interpretations and Idiosyncratic Ideas

There were others, four percent of the respondents, who had developed a much stricter attitude and who appeared to find that sin was a very real and troubling part of their lives.

> If the Bible says it's sin, it's simply sin.
>
> I have learned that there were sins that I hadn't known were sins before. These were things that I had done and planned on doing again.
>
> Now I know that if you only think about it you are committing a sin. I used to feel sin was just something you did wrong. Now I feel sometimes a sin can be when you don't do something right.
>
> I think we commit a lot more sins than we realize.
>
> I have done a lot of sinning in the last four years.
>
> It looks like I commit sin everyday.
>
> The more things I do it seems like they're sinful.

Finally, there is a small group of responses that are so individual that there is a temptation to give them more importance than they probably warrant. However, at least a few of them should be noted because of the insight they offer into the thinking of certain teens:

> Sin, to me, is just a concept conceived by man in order to relate with God, the afterlife (assuming there is one) and his fellow men.
>
> There is no such thing as sin. An individual can sin against others but he cannot sin against himself.
>
> Sin is not as bad as I thought. It's almost like a growth experience. I used to believe I would be struck by lightning, so to speak, but know that won't happen now.

> I now feel that God doesn't know if we sin, so sin isn't important. Who is God to tell us what's right and what's wrong?

Even among these negative remarks, however, there are those that offer reason for encouragement because these young men and women are wrestling with difficult ideas, which they usually do not fully comprehend. They feel that it is their responsibility to find their way through the confusion and they are in desperate need of better guides and better guidelines than they seem to have been offered. Even the awareness that no one has an easy answer, and that it is better to join together in the search rather than to launch out alone into the wilderness, could give them the security that they need to hold on to their faith, even though the thread at times may appear to have broken. If they have a right foundation they have a better chance of finding understanding, compassion and forgiveness in the future.

One student, self-described as a practicing Catholic, wrote:

> I challenge the idea of sin itself. If man is a product of *heredity* and his *environment,* where does "self" emerge? Also, I feel that people always do the best they can, and if God knows this, how can sin exist? What is sin? A punishable act of evil? Punishment from an unconditionally loving God? God is not human. Punishment is a release of anger. Rationalization makes it an attempt to teach others to do what is right. No! I feel that if a person does wrong, he does it either unknowingly or uncontrollably . . . if God is so forgiving, punishment is contradictory.

It is a matter of great concern that obviously serious students should fail to comprehend the notion that a loving God can punish for willful transgressions, just as loving parents can punish their children when they do wrong, while at the same time encouraging them to reach the point at which they will want to do what is right without having the threat of punishment as a spur. These same students probably do not question the need for rules in sports, and are unlikely to think that each player on a football team should be free to make his own decisions. Yet they reject the authority of the church on matters of far greater importance. This suggests that there may be a deep misunderstanding not only of *what* the church teaches, but *why* and *how* it teaches.

> I realized that most rules and regulations in the church were made by men. Before we had been taught that everything in the Church was God's will. How can the men who made up these rules be sure that they follow God's will?"

This comment reminds us of the confusion that is shown also by many adults who find it hard to distinguish between fundamental doctrine and the rules imposed by the Church over the centuries which may have been designed to meet conditions that no longer exist and which may be changed or modified.

Conclusion

Two easy reactions are possible to the opinions of these students: to take the authoritarian line that "there are these rules that they must obey, and if they don't they cannot call themselves Catholic," or alternatively, "the Church is changing and is no longer in a position to establish and enforce hard and fast rules." Neither response seemed correct.

There is open and honest disagreement over some Church laws. Current statistics indicate that the majority of married Catholics practice some form of artificial birth control without feeling that this removes them from the Church. The whole question of celibacy, a matter of regulation rather than of dogma, has been discussed at great length. It would therefore be hypocritical to say that adults may have their own dissenting opinions on these and other matters, but that teens must swallow the thing whole.

The difficulties arise when we try to decide which freedoms should be given up, and it is not surprising that so many of these students were fighting for their right to fulfill their current sexual desires, this being a natural preoccupation for their age. A businessman might prefer to keep all his profits for himself rather than pay taxes to support the poor. The old and the ill have been known to claim the right to end their lives.

Perhaps the greatest challenge to the parents and teachers of religion in Catholic schools and parishes is to make this a subject of such immediate personal interest and concern that the young will be able to make it a real part of their lives rather than an abstract idea.

Topics for Discussion

1. To what extent is it possible or desirable to expect young people to adhere to a strict moral code?

2. How can parents and teachers successfully instill an awareness of sin that will avoid unnecessary guilt while encouraging the need to strive for improvement?

3. How can the laws of God be opposed to the permissiveness of the world in a positive way?

4. How can the Church resurrect the Sacrament of Reconciliation?

7
THE CHURCH AND RELIGION

> Nothing is really done to help teenagers in the Catholic church. Our Church leaders need to realize that we are the future church and they should try harder to reach out and understand us.

A Gallup Report on Religion in America, published in March 1984, although not dealing exclusively with Catholics, confirmed some of the findings of the present study:

> Teens are clearly searching for spiritual meanings in their lives with a new intensity. . . . Despite the growing interest among teens in religious and spiritual matters, many teenagers remain "turned off" by churches and organized religion. They are, nevertheless, highly religious in certain key respects (p. 64).

Some of the responses in the *Gallup Report* were close to those already noted, with 95 percent of the respondents believing in God and 87 percent saying that they pray. Gallup also notes the lack of a fully developed prayer life, ignorance of Scripture and "the inability to develop the discipline necessary to support a commitment consistent with religious experience and belief," and comments that it seems teenagers are "not finding the spiritual dimensions they seek in their traditional religious upbringing."

This lack of discipline is linked to impatience when they find things not to their liking, and may be related to an apparent failure in their religious education, which has left them without a firm grounding in church doctrine and an almost total ignorance (at least as demonstrated by the responses of these students) of church history. This is especially clear in their attitude toward the church as a worldwide institution, which is the subject of this chapter.

Student Responses

Only 30 percent of those questioned believed that most Catholics practice what they are taught by the church, while 14 percent believe that Catholics are required to accept everything that the pope says, although one explained:

> I believe in the pope as the leader of our church, but from what I have learned in Religion, I am not to believe that he is always infallible. I also think that the church's rules must, like all other concepts, change as the times change. I do not believe that the church can apply its old rules to twentieth century society without some revision.

Sixty percent thought that the church should take an active stand against such groups as the Nazi party, communists and the KKK, while 59 percent said that the church should take public stands on important political issues, such as the nuclear arms race, busing for school integration, equal rights, etc. On the other hand, there were those who took issue with the church's teaching on social justice and thought that it should not become involved in politics:

The Church & Religion

> I don't think the church should stand up for certain things in the government because it has such a powerful influence and millions of brain-washed followers.

> I believe the church as a whole should stop getting involved in political affairs. I know sometimes they do it to stop the injustices to the poor, but this makes matters worse.

Others thought it ignored topics on which it has, in fact, spoken clearly:

> I feel strongly that the church should get much more involved in political issues — taking stands on issues would put the church back into people's lives.

At the time of the survey, the Bishops' Pastoral on War and Peace had not yet been published in its final form, but was the subject of considerable discussion in both the Catholic and secular press. There could be no denying that this qualified as a "controversial stand," and certainly it offered leadership and guidance, but this student did not seem to be aware of it. Other respondents expressed a desire for leadership, even though the right to dissent was also valued:

> I feel the church must modernize itself to the changing world. They must get out and do more in the community. They must take controversial stands on controversial issues. If Catholics disagree with the stand they take, it is no sin, but at least there will be some show of leadership and guidance from a semi-trusted source.

When teenagers moved from the church's involvement in politics and world affairs to its influence on their own lives, their criticisms became more emphatic. Peer pressure played a role in their response to the church:

> My friends are not totally separated from the church, but they are a little more distant than when they were younger. A lot of times it is peer pressure. If somebody doesn't really have the religious conviction in their life, they may feel uncomfortable with it.

Others spoke of the difference between merely attending religion classes and actually believing:

> Our religion is often preached but not practiced.
>
> I feel religion is a belief and not an obligation, and that is why there are so many different religions and controversies between the churches.

The Church in History

The lack of any historical perspective was illustrated by one student who criticized the Church for being based on communist beliefs, which is a startling example of history turned topsy-turvy. Others thought that decisions made only 20 years earlier were already outdated:

> I think that the church's views of the world are far behind. They are trying to apply standards to today's world that were relevant 10 to 20 years ago but are in head-on conflict with the world today. It should try to understand the younger generation and listen to what they are saying, why many of them rebel against the church.

While the institutional church can sometimes be faulted for considering all change in terms of progress over several centuries, young people are not likely to achieve very much by demanding that a span of 20 years be accepted as a measure of obsolescence. In fact, conservative church leaders could use such expectations as evidence of a lack of understanding and the constructive suggestions that were also made could be thrown out at the same time.

With few exceptions, these students were asking the church to move in the direction of greater freedom. A few were opposed to change, while welcoming open discussion:

> I hope the church never gets to a point where it compromises its ideas so it will fit in.

> The Catholic Church, I believe, is the most relevant religious institution in the world today. As such, it should endeavor to propagate the faith in an honest, realistic manner, open to discussion of issues of the day and the different circumstances that affect the world (and not only Catholics). However, it should *not* deviate from its traditionalist approach or its strict emphasis on certain moral issues, no matter what the pressures may be.

A girl from a middle-class family made the observation that "the church can help by staying the same." She believed that the changes of Vatican II had made the church relevant, that it should retain the substance but perhaps make use of new media. A second student, the daughter of professional parents, said that the church should be able to change to meet people's needs, that tradition is important but that the main thing is to communicate with people.

Some of the "traditional" students were more emphatic in their opinions:

> I just don't understand, if we are supposed to be receiving the bread and wine of Jesus, why isn't it just the priest who passes it out? Why does it have

to be normal people? That's like giving up something we believe in. Everything is changing. Things should remain the same, just like Jesus wanted it.

The church to me stands for God and when we allow man to make decisions, our problems occur. People don't follow the Bible because they feel it is too exaggerated. They say, "That's not what God meant." They think that a group of people got together and wrote this book.

I think that young people especially need a stable church, one that is open but not too "modern." Believe it or not, we like tradition and the "new" church sometimes turns us off or makes us lose respect (in a sense) for the Church. Hopefully, a happy medium can be attained and the church can be a meaningful and relevant part of everyone's life.

One teenager faulted both the Catholic press and teachers for the confusion:

Some of the publications which claim to report the Church are very mistaken. *L'Osservatore Romano* is by far the one I know that is very reliable — it reprints word for word the pope's letters and addresses. The local Catholic newspapers seem to reword and distort the pope's statements. The religious education programs are sadly lacking. You don't learn what the Church says and has taught for centuries. It's words, nothings. It's confusing to the few people who have been blessed with knowing, people who are in touch with the truths taught for centuries. The others become disoriented and frustrated . . . the teachers themselves seem to be overcome by it, contradicting themselves and saying that your parents don't know anything.

This statement echoes those made in certain highly traditional publications. However, it must be admitted that there is a good deal of truth in what they say about the failure of both education and communication, and it is unfortunate that their generally strident tone often means that they are discounted by many moderate as well as liberal Catholics. It is certainly true that if teachers have a poor understanding of church doctrine and are themselves confused and uncertain, they will not be able to convince their inquiring and skeptical students.

Desire for Change

A far larger number of respondents were in favor of change — it often seemed, the more the better. Their comments reflect a failure to understand, on even the most elementary level, that an institution cannot be judged on the extent to which it "changes with the times," or to consider the possibility that society might be wrong and that the Church, as reflected in its basic teachings, doctrine and faith, could be right. A frantic effort to keep up with the latest fad is usually a sign of weakness rather than of strength. These students were children of the post-Vatican II church, too young to appreciate from personal experience the changes that occurred in the immediate aftermath of the council. However, they were aware that change took place then and seemed to believe that this should, if anything, accelerate rather than slow down.

The students failed to relate their concept of God and prayer to the need for a structured religion. There was the sense that they saw religion as a compulsory course in school rather than as a commitment to a way of life and that they almost divorced it from a relationship with God:

> I feel that there is a better way of getting to heaven than joining a religion.

76 Faith Without Form

> I don't feel religion is all that necessary. A person can still lead a good life without it. . . . I feel I've been overburdened with religion. From teachers I have learned much about the Bible and philosophical ideas, but religion still remains something I must study and church a place I must go to on Sunday mornings.

> The church, I believe, is out of touch with the real society. Their teachings are still a lot old-fashioned; they have not changed with the times. The priests I relate to seem to be in good touch with reality. It's the higher-up priests who don't understand today's people, their feelings, beliefs, concerns, etc.

> I believe the Church has a lot of changes to make. Many people in today's society are falling from the Church because of its medieval ideas. I think I would become more involved with the Church again if it changed.

Is the Church Necessary?

As a result, certain teenagers felt that the Church was unnecessary and that they did not need its help:

> I believe a person can be good and honest without the Church. I have nothing against it and I admire people who express sincere faith. The Church is merely an institution to me. I think a person should learn to depend on herself before an institution.

> I believe that most people who attend church do not do it because they want to, but because of pressure outside the Church, such as upbringing and society. People today have the option of not belonging to a religion because, unlike years ago, it is not as important.

Many teenagers seemed to feel little loyalty as Catholics and were perfectly willing to shop around among the various denominations in search of the one that would best meet their needs:

> I do not feel that Catholics should have to follow every rule set down by the Church. If they love God and help others but do not go to church every Sunday, then that should be OK. Also, if a Catholic wants to attend a Mass for another faith, then that should be OK too. After all, is *God* Catholic?

Freedom to Choose

Not unexpectedly, 95 percent felt that they should be allowed to make their own decisions on whether to belong to the Church. The responses ranged from those who expected to continue as Catholics to those who saw a great many choices before them:

> I think in terms of religion I will always be a Catholic. I may not practice faithfully because the Church is not interesting to me, but I think I will always believe in God and remain in the religion.

> I think people should be encouraged to seek out other ideals and ways. Let the God of their choosing decide the way for them. And let me decide for myself and you too. For there are many ways to the right way! Who has the right to say which one is correct? Only God does! He showed me this way and personally tells everyone else.

> I have recently been in contact with several Episcopalians and was impressed with their beliefs. My church seems to be very shallow.

> I am a Catholic but I don't think that this religion

is the right one for me. I still feel that there is something missing. I have been to a few other churches and they weren't what I was looking for either. I need to find a church where I can feel security and warmth and where I don't feel pressured or that it is a routine or chore to go.

Relationship with the Church

If students want to make up their own minds about religion, it is inevitable that this will affect their feelings about the institutional Church. Unlike the student quoted at the beginning of this chapter, the majority did not think of themselves as "the Church." Although they claimed a close personal friendship with God, their relationship with the Church was decidedly frosty. They perceived it as an aloof, intimidating and irrelevant entity, presumably made up of bishops and other members of the hierarchy who seemed to have little interest in or understanding of young people.

This impression did not spring up, fully developed, as they approached graduation, but had to develop almost imperceptibly from their years of watching and absorbing the attitudes and examples of their families, teachers, fellow parishioners and peers. What these people *did* was more important than what they *said,* even though there may have been no conscious realization of this.

If children grow up hearing criticism of the Church, of the bishops' statements or of their pastor's call for concern for the poor, this will influence their own behavior, whether they choose to accept or reject their parents' point of view. This was realized by the student who said:

> Many of my peers do things only for themselves. Therefore I don't think the Church should try to bend too far backwards for these teenagers. They don't

like anyone telling them what to do. I feel that the
parents are the ones who should be educated more
in raising their children to be good Catholics. I know
I follow the Church strongly because of my parents'
attitudes.

There were also those whose positive feelings toward the Church had grown out of their family background, such as the girl who said that it was the Church that had taught her why she was here. She had gone to church for as long as she could remember and always attended Catholic schools. She felt that they had taught her about God and helped her to make the right decisions about religion, saying:

The Church tells us about what Jesus did down here
and that he is our example. All you have to do is
follow that example, which helps you to care for other
people. Going to church is a chance, at least for an
hour, to get my mind cleared of everything and just
concentrate on God.

The same student thought that the church is sensitive to people's needs, but that it takes a while for it to react because it is such an old institution:

You can see that things have changed. People said
you couldn't understand the Latin Mass, so that
changed gradually and finally we don't have Latin
Mass.

Several areas were selected for criticism — in particular, the Church's authority to teach. When students questioned the teaching of doctrine they were often on shaky ground:

I believe that the church doesn't have the right to
govern our lives. They can voice their opinions on

80 Faith Without Form

what is wrong or right. But they can't say that something *is* right or *is* wrong, and if we do what they say is wrong, they can't call that a sin.

For the church to become more in touch with the youth of the 1980's I feel that it should direct its attention away from the strict doctrine it always has been noted for and center itself upon people today.

Church Authority

There was a widespread sense that the church was too authoritarian and the teenagers pushed against this:

I feel that the Catholic church tries to force people to live in a way that it feels that people should live, whether it is against what they believe or not.

It seems that every time the Church wants to make a stand it maneuvers the people by bringing religion into it, making it a big moral issue and telling everyone how they should believe and that if they don't they are wrong in the eyes of God. I don't think this is right. Every person has a personal opinion and there might be good reasons for it.

These and other comments create a strong impression that the students have not learned to differentiate between the doctrine of the church, the core elements of faith that are essential if one is to call oneself Catholic, and the various laws, traditions, customs and habits that have multiplied over the centuries. Some of these have acquired great weight because they have been accepted by the faithful for so long; others were introduced as a matter of administrative convenience or to meet the customs of a certain period, and can therefore be changed without affecting the church's credibility. It is naive to think that because Catholics were once required to abstain from meat on

Fridays but are now allowed to eat it, that this also means that belief in the divinity of Christ is equally a matter of personal convenience, or that relaxation of the rules for fasting before communion means that they are now free to rewrite the creed to suit their own tastes.

Where there was a conflict between the teaching of the church and the inclination of the individual, the church was likely to be the loser:

> The basic problem is that the church hasn't changed its role or ideas, and since the kids today are products of the 1960s, many people do not accept them. So they have been doing their own thing on abortion, birth control and others which they think is right.
>
> I feel that the church is out of touch with the younger society now. They condemn our every movement.
>
> It is sometimes very difficult to abide by the rules of the Catholic church. At times I feel like changing to another religion because of my strong disapproval of the ways of the Catholic church. I'm not going to risk hurting myself because of rules and standards set by the Catholic church. My friends ask me why I don't have anything to back up these rules.

They allowed the church very limited authority:

> The church, as it seems to me, is just an old institution. It expects people to live by morals that are outdated. The growth of science, technology has cast doubt on the legitimacy of the church. It takes away freedom from the individual and leaves guilt on a person. It often says something, yet gives no logical reason why it is wrong — and often, when in a corner, a person will defend his argument and the church by saying, "have faith." To me this is the number

one cop-out. It is a human institution, run by humans, and is therefore fallible, so why should I feel guilt when, in the end, the Church may have been wrong all along? The Bible, I feel, is not absolutely wrong, but throughout the years it has been interpreted so many different ways that it's hard to find the real meaning.

Despite the students' criticism of the church they apparently have no desire to change the method of religious instruction by actually teaching religion themselves. Sixty-eight percent of the students indicated no interest in teaching religion; only 16 percent responded favorably and the other 15 percent had no opinion.

"Custom-made" Catholicism

Many students believed that they could more or less design their own "Catholicism":

> I feel I am a practicing Catholic. I go to church. I accept communion. I pray and look to God and church for blessings and comfort and strength. However, sometimes I have a hard time believing everything I was taught and also I have, as I've grown up, developed my own insights to sin, love, premarital sex, abortion, etc. A lot of the time I feel I don't believe what the Catholic church does, but I don't think that makes me a non-Catholic.

> Although I'm not involved in my church I have strong beliefs and faith, which is enough for me right now.

> I am a very firm believer in God and what he preaches, but I feel that my communication or relationship with God is not evident only by Church. To be honest, church really bores me. I don't get

much out of it. But God knows that I love and respect him. I don't think he's offended if I miss Mass. My relationship with God is between me and God. Nobody else.

I believe that the way a person would prefer to practice religion should be left up to them. Yes, there should be different denominations, to be used as guidelines only. A person should not be considered a sinner or unholy if he does not practice the beliefs that his religion has. The choice should be left up to the person. The church's views should be just that, a view, not a law or rule to follow.

I feel religion is a very personal thing. What I believe and how I practice it is my business. I like to share my beliefs with others, but not push them on others.

It is true that many young people are shying away from the church. My main emphasis is the fact that I feel religious believers should be guided in their moral decisions by their church. I do not think it necessary to believe every single word that the church says. Instead, being rational human beings, I think that we should be given the right to choose what we, ourselves, want to believe. I feel that the parish member should have a say in what the church decides.

The Church and God

The lack of understanding that the structure of the Church plays an important role in one's personal relationship with God, together with the belief that an institutional church was not necessary, is illustrated by this comment:

To me, being a good Catholic means not living by

the rules of being a good Catholic, but living the way Christ did — loving other people.

The church can hardly be blamed for those who reject it for essentially selfish reasons, but it could use some self-examination concerning those who want to believe and belong but feel that they are being rejected or are not receiving the support that they look for:

> If the Church is to get in touch with young adults, it must make a stronger effort. The problems young people face must also be considered when trying to start a communication.
>
> I believe the Church should be more open and try to help people who are confused and have problems dealing with these issues (birth control, homosexuality and abortion) rather than just setting up rigid guidelines that make people feel guilty. Personally, I don't like to get preached at and I resent the church calling me a bad Catholic just because I disagree with certain issues. For example, I know of "good" Catholics that go to church on Sunday but act like beasts from Monday through Saturday. Because of this I feel comfortable with (my) relationship with God, because I at least know that I'm trying to be a good person and that's really what it's all about.

Teenagers may feel that they have all the answers, but they are open to reasonable explanations. If they understand that there are certain beliefs that are not open to discussion because they are beyond human comprehension and must therefore be accepted as matters of faith, they are less likely to lose their bearings when they look at the changes that have been made in other areas and will be able to judge these as part of the continuing growth of a living church.

Like intelligent adolescents down the centuries, these students want people (the church) to level with them, to explain the reasons why they are being asked to do certain things, to believe certain things. They resent being simply told that they must accept what their teachers or their priests tell them, without discussion. They have legitimate questions, new to them although many of their parents and grandparents would recognize them from their own youth, and they are asking that these questions be treated seriously. If there is no simple answer, they respond much better to an honest admission of confusion or ignorance than an attempt to browbeat them into acceptance by a show of authority. No one is going to remain a convinced Catholic simply because their parents or teachers ordered them to do so:

> I don't feel that the Catholic church is being a guide to us. It just seems like a realm of power. I just don't feel the concern coming from the religious people like I feel they should give us. They should be supportive, not dictative.

Alienation

The comments made by some students suggested that they were so out of sympathy with the Church that they had effectively removed themselves from its influence:

> I feel that if a person does not go to church but tries to be a good Christian, they are not doing wrong. I try my best to do right and I know sometimes I'm wrong, but I feel that church really does nothing for me. The only reason I go is because my parents go and I feel that when I live under their roof I do what they want. At least, most of the time.
>
> The Church is a hypocritical institution that makes

rules, alienates God and doesn't practice what it preaches.

I believe that the state of the church is in poor shape. I am not an atheist. I believe in some higher being. I want to believe, but I think the Church has not helped me in understanding.

This removal from active church involvement was sometimes associated with the rejection of any formal religion, perhaps most strongly expressed by the student who said that he believed he was going to heaven "no matter what." He felt that there was no reason to go to church if you don't want to and admitted that he hated Sundays but particularly hated having to "interrupt" Christmas morning in order to go to church. He quoted his father as having said, "No son of mine will be an atheist or embarrass me by going to hell."

Some of the students felt that any failure in faith rested not with the church but in themselves, because they experienced difficulty in measuring up to expectations:

Many teenagers do not feel they are good enough for the church. Yet they do not recognize the whole purpose of the person Jesus. This is a large problem.

I used to go to Mass every Sunday and try to obey all of the commandments, but I can't really blame anyone for me not going now. . . . I just didn't get enough support from family and friends.

I feel the church is more of a refuge from the turmoil outside. I do believe, but practicing all that is expected of me is very difficult. I realize we all have to get involved and give of ourselves. It is impossible for me to do this, therefore I feel I have pinpointed the major problem I have with the Catholic church.

In contrast another student said:

> I'm very glad that the church makes a stand on certain issues that concern us as Catholics. I find it very important for people to look toward the church for guidance. I have found that most teenagers or people I know go to church and practice Christianity because they choose to believe in God and what the Catholic religion stands for. Before, I felt like I was distant and separated from the church, but then I realized that the Church has its arms extended to anyone and everyone — you just have to want it.

The Mass

One area in which their dissatisfaction was especially noticeable was in their comments on the Mass. Those which we consider here concern the basic nature of the Mass rather than their experience in their own parishes, which will be dealt with in the next chapter.

Whether they wanted to keep the Mass the way it is, revert to the older forms, or introduce radical changes, few students seemed to understand what the Mass really is or its importance in the life of a believer:

> The importance of Mass has not been stressed in my life — I do not have a clear understanding of it. To me Mass is a traditional ceremony of something that happened thousands of years ago. When I came to the point where I had the Mass memorized, I began to cease going.

> The Mass is extremely formal and I find it hard to relate.

> In what I consider the older Mass, it was more a matter of worshiping God, and now it's putting on a

> show. Frankly, that's an insult to my intelligence. It's just distracting, there are too many people around the altar.

One student said, "Vatican II should be cited more often in Masses, not just the Old Testament." If he was speaking of the liturgy and not the homily, this was another example of ignorance of what the Mass actually is and of the difference between a centuries-old sacrifice and the council documents, vitally important as these are.

Some students seemed to regard the requirement of attendance at Mass as an almost intolerable restriction on their freedom:

> Some people feel really restricted by the Church. If it is absolutely necessary to go to Sunday Mass, that affects their freedom, because some people have other things that they want to do, other things that they have to do. If the Church says that they have to go to Mass they lose respect for it, because they can see ways of getting around having to do this. The Mass is losing its meaning. I can understand what the Church stands for, but the Mass is just going through the motions. It doesn't seem important, as long as you know what it's about and what you should do.

Conclusion

From what these teenagers say about the church, it seems that they have a key misunderstanding of the church's role, in thinking that it should be prepared to change its basic teachings to meet the expectations of today's society. In an increasingly secular and materialistic culture, most of them do not look to the church for example, support and strength. Instead they seek to change it to fit their own wishes — even if this involves creating an essentially new religion which some continue to call "Catholicism." Others, more perceptive, admit that they can no longer see themselves as part of the church. Still others hope to find a means of reconciliation:

> I think it's about time for something to be done about the rift between teens and the church. My opinion is that although the church is necessary in many ways, many teens don't think that the church's beliefs on sex and marriage are relevant to society today, so they don't participate in the church or its beliefs.

Very few teenagers have contact with bishops or cardinals, or spend their time reading pastorals or encyclicals. The place, apart from their family, where they absorb their understanding of religion and the church is in the local parish, which is what many of them mean when they speak of "The Church." Whether their parishes are giving them what they want or, more importantly, what they need, is something that will be examined in the next chapter.

Topics for Discussion

1. What steps could be taken by both the church and its leaders and the teenagers to heal the rift between them?

2. Why is religious history important to the development of young Catholics, and how should it be taught?

3. What steps can the Church take to recognize the difference in today's youth, who are half-adult, half-child?

4. How do we explain to youth the contradiction of the Church's current political activism vs. constitutional separation of Church and State?

5. What are the major changes in society and in the Catholic

90 Faith Without Form

Church over the past 20 years, and how do these affect the adult population?

6. To what extent can teenagers be expected to understand the causes of these changes and appreciate the reactions of those who lived through them?

8
THE PARISH COMMUNITY

I think sometimes the trouble with the church is that on a local level it has trouble dealing with an intelligent person with insight.

If the typical teenager saw the universal church as an institution in which they played no active part, the local church affected their lives more directly but, unfortunately, often in negative ways.

The Mass

The Mass was the central and sometimes the only point of contact with the parish and they did not hesitate to criticize:

I've lost interest in Masses, they do bore me. I still believe and try to live a Christian life, but I don't go to Mass faithfully any more.

The students showed little evidence that they considered the Mass to be an important part of their lives.

Sometimes I have the desire to go to church and then other times I just don't have any desire to go. Some-

> times when I do go it seems as though my mind wanders around to other things. I have problems sometimes concentrating on the Mass.

There were those who felt that the Mass was less appealing than their other weekend activities.

> It doesn't bother me to go to Mass, but sometimes you have other things you would like to do, or you wouldn't mind just relaxing.

They showed little understanding of the significance of the Mass and, as a result, there were complaints that the liturgy followed the same pattern and that the same prayers were said each week:

> I have been attending Mass weekly since I was in first grade. I feel that the same readings are used at the same time of the year and you hear the same homily after them. Because of my upbringing I feel terrible if I'm not sick and I do not attend Mass, but it becomes a ritual of saying the same thing week after week.

> Mass is so routine. It's like there is no feeling at all. There aren't any personal kinds of touches in Mass. Every week is the same thing. Mass makes God seem so far away and out of reach.

It is sad that anyone should see the Mass as a barrier between people and God, but there is no doubt that the manner in which it is celebrated can make a great deal of difference in how the congregation responds. Unfortunately, there are too many churches in which there is rarely any sense of "celebration." If the priest, for whatever reason — overwork, preoccupation with other problems, lack of enthusiasm or his own loss of a sense of mystery — treats the Mass as a routine or something to be got out of the way as soon as possible, there is little chance that the congregation will experience it as life-enhancing or as an opportunity to communicate with God. The students sensed this, although they did not necessarily understand the causes of the problem:

> I feel that if priests, in general, would make their homilies and services more interesting, people would come to Mass more often. People feel that Mass is boring because there is nothing to hold their interest.

We need only compare the atmosphere of a Mass celebrated by a priest who is conscious of the enormous significance of re-enacting Christ's sacrifice and one by a priest who has lost this sense of awe and is merely going through the motions to realize that this is not a matter of dreaming up novel ways of approaching the liturgy. While there are now more options available and many acceptable sytles, from the gospel Mass to the austere monastic celebration, if the priest has forgotten, even briefly, the meaning of his priesthood, the Mass will be lacking this esstential quality and in consequence will speak less effectively to the people.

Other students were disturbed by the attitudes of the adult congregation and as a result questioned the importance of participation in the Mass:

> Maybe it's the parish I go to, but I get frustrated because it seems that half the people don't care, and the other half are so taken up in it that it's almost false. It really bothers me. It seems that there's a Sunday morning burst of faith, but just forget the other six days. On Sunday morning you're there cheering God on. I think God would be embarrassed.
>
> When I go to Mass it seems that everybody's there

all dressed up just for appearance. If there was a Mass with just 10 people, if it was concentrated, I think I would get a lot more out of it, but I go there and everyone's rich and looks at each other and tries to outdo each other. I think most everybody wants to appear to be well off and at Mass everybody is looking around and not trying to concentrate.

Another student also said that people came in their best clothes and seemed to like to show off. Nobody talked to anybody and the handshake they gave was so cold that he grew to hate the church.

There is sometimes a fine line between wearing "best clothes" out of respect for the importance of the occasion and doing so to impress one's neighbors. At the opposite extreme we see instances of young and not so young people who seem to have come to church straight from repairing the car, or who stroll up the aisle to receive communion as casually as if they were getting a soda.

This problem was summed up by the student who said:

I feel that every time I go to church it is just a routine act which I get nothing out of. I look around and see that not many people really care what is going on. The priests do not look like they really care about what they are doing. I cannot say that I look forward to going to church on Sunday and I never really get anything out of it at all. I am positive in my belief in God but feel that I can be closer to him when I am outside of church or any kind of prayer group.

What these student responses seem to illustrate is a collision between the style of the pre- and post-Vatican II church, complicated by the fact that there is no clean-cut dividing line between the two. Age is not a deciding factor. There are elderly priests and laity who have embraced the changes with enthusiasm, while some young priests and laity yearn to return to the old ways. There are parishes where priests who regret the changes of Vatican II are ministering to parishioners who want to take advantage of all the possibilities offered, just as there are other parishes where the priest is struggling to pull the people, kicking and screaming, into the modern church, as well as any number of permutations between these extremes. Not many parishes are made up entirely of like-minded parishioners, so there will always be some who are unhappy; and every time a new pastor is appointed the entire structure of the parish is liable to change.

Idealistic adolescents, still believing in the possibility of perfection, look at this confusion and are dismayed and critical. They have not reached the point where they are able to separate the ideal from the actual and to worship God in whatever setting is offered. They are not to be blamed for this. More and more adults are leaving their home parish in search of a community which provides them with the style of worship they prefer. While they may agree, in theory, that it would be preferable to remain and work to bring about change in their own parish, they find many obstacles to this — a pastor who is not about to cooperate, or a majority of parishioners who are content with things as they are. The dissatisfied come from all points on the spectrum and include those who are still looking for a Tridentine Mass, those trying to avoid the kiss of peace and those looking for its more enthusiastic expression, those who prefer to be quiet and those who want to sing loudly at every opportunity.

Most of the teenagers in the study were still locked in to their home parishes, although some suspected that there might be alternatives:

> In some cases I haven't been pleased with the sermons that some priests give on Sunday. But in such

> a case I went to a different church that I could better relate to. So I never gave up on the church because of Masses that I can't relate to.
>
> I don't know if my feelings would be any different if I belonged to a different church, but I don't feel very close to mine. I think it seems like a clique.
>
> Our town parish seems to be very uncaring and regimented. It has discouraged people from coming to church. The pastor acts like he owns the place. That has had a major effect on my attitudes about religion and the church, which I think is too bad. It should be more of a community.

A male student believed that the Mass is "more attuned to adults" and suggested that teens would understand it more if it was in their own language. While there are limits to the ways in which the liturgy can be adapted, homilies at youth Masses offer an excellent opportunity for this type of communication, particularly if the young people themselves are encouraged to take part in the discussion.

Homilies

There can be no doubt that the priest has a tremendous influence on the character of the parish and one of the most public examples of this influence is the Sunday homily. Teenagers are not alone in finding much to criticize:

> When I go to church at my parish, the priest always lectures. I really feel bad saying this about a priest, but he really acts as if he is so much better than anyone else. He gets everyone so mad. I used to enjoy going to church until he came. So did my family, but not any more. This one priest really ruins it for everybody. I know a lot of people who have stopped going

to church because of him.

> A lot of times the homilies are excessively boring. It seems that the priest just keeps talking and talking, without getting to a specific point. Sometimes it will be good, but a lot of times it will just be somebody talking. I don't know what can be done about this, because something different appeals to each person.

> Although I've known some really nice priests, my pastor is totally out of touch with younger and older people alike. My family avoids going to Masses he may say at all costs. He rambles on and on about things with no relevance to the contemporary. He is authoritative also.

One young woman agreed that "it depends on the priest," saying that she had been to some services where the priest was very good, but that the pastor of her church "tends to preach down. He'll point out all the evils but won't say one good thing. He says that teenagers are too involved in premarital sex, while another priest will tell you that it's wrong but will explain and talk to you like a human person."

Hanging In

Some students were prepared to hang on in spite of difficulties:

> I don't know how many young people go to church just because their parents are making them or if they really believe in it. A lot of my friends go to the same parish that I do and I see them there. Maybe they have drifted, but they are still sticking with going to Mass. I think the homilies are a little bit above us right now.

There were also students who were fortunate in their parishes and spoke well of their experiences:

> The church offers a lot of hope. When you enter the church you feel different, you feel like a new person. If the priest sits down and talks to a person, that can help a whole lot. It doesn't matter if he talks to a group or individually, as long as he gets across.
>
> I go to church on Sundays, but if I had something I wanted to do, like shopping, I used to think it was OK to miss church. Now I go every Sunday and make a point that I don't miss. Masses are practically all the same. They read out of a book, but some of the priests talk to us in their own words about the Bible, so that kids can understand it, and that's what I think is good. If you're not participating, your mind wanders.
>
> I think church has become more important in my life since I made the decision to go. I enjoy going to Mass. I plan to continue going. I can't think of anything that I would want to change. It picks me up, makes me feel good, being with God for that time and knowing that he's still there.

Sacrament of Reconciliation (Confession) and Church Discipline

There were only a few comments on other aspects of parish life, but these included some negative comments on confession:

> I don't believe in going to confession. I feel that it's between you and God, and the priest shouldn't be involved. The reason why I went was because I was made to go at my grade school. I didn't understand

and was really afraid of God.

> I guess the last time I went to confession was about three years ago. The priest started yelling at me, raising his voice. I didn't go there to get yelled at. He is supposed to help me and tell me ways to ask for forgiveness, not to tell me I was a bad girl. I know I did something wrong, that is why I was there. If that is how it will be, I won't go.

There were also complaints about church discipline when this conflicted with personal opinions:

> I think that the church is too ceremonial. Too many strict standards that must be followed. For example, at my church if you want to get married in the church, you must notify the parish six months in advance and begin marriage classes. I think this is ridiculous. Maybe an interview and a discussion with the couple, but to have to take classes to get married doesn't make sense.

Criticisms and Suggestions

There were also more valid complaints:

> I think that the Catholic church is becoming too involved in government and not with the people who need it. I visited my pastor and he didn't do me any good. It was a total waste of my time. He listened to me in one ear and out the other. My church only has the parishioners for the money they need. My God doesn't live with a money changer on his belt, in a vault or bank.

> There are some priests who are always doing everything, Boy Scouts and this and this. You could never catch them if you tried.

It was apparent that the majority of these teenagers did not see themselves as active members of their parish communities, able to become involved and initiate change. A few did offer suggestions:

> Priests could be more counselors and be available to listen.

> The church could help if teens had someone to talk to, to tell them, "It's not your fault, you couldn't help what happened."

> I think there should be a lot more activities within the parish for young adults. In this way they will learn about God and always be in touch with him and not be so alienated from the church. There is a problem in today's society that if "everyone" is not doing something, then no one will participate.

> If religion could be offered in a more casual setting to relate it with our daily lives, I think teenagers would be able to relate better.

Yet even here there is no indication of any willingness to work on parish programs, but an expectation that someone else, probably the priest, should arrange for these activities to be made available, with no effort on the part of the recipients. It is a "give me" mentality. It is not a surprising attitude in a society that attempts to judge how much its children are loved by the number of things that are given to them.

Priests, Brothers and Sisters

While it is true that the pastor is the ultimate authority in the parish and that not all pastors are perfect, most hardly deserve such severe criticism as these students leveled at them:

> I believe the ideals of the church should change with the times. What turns people off is that the priests are like the parishioners. They are hypocrites; they preach one thing and practice another.
>
> I do not like the way the priests live. They can drink, which should not be allowed. Most of them are very phoney and unconcerned.
>
> The rectory was filthy rich, rolling in money.

Because priests, together with brothers and sisters, have dedicated their lives to God they are expected to be perfect. They are in a no-win situation, because whether they are open about their humanity or try to appear to be without fault, they can be accused of hypocrisy, at least by some of the teenagers:

> The priests I know are very phoney.
>
> The Catholic church to me seems very out of touch. I do believe in God and I pray often, but when I go to church everything seems so artificial and fake. The priests, nuns, bishops and even the pope seem to try and give us a "perfect" image of themselves. But they're not — they are human and have as many faults as any other person. The only perfect being is God and no one can ever be exactly like him.

It will probably take some time for them to learn to be as tolerant and forgiving toward others, particularly those in authority, as they already are toward themselves.

Yet there are contradictions in the data. Two items in the questionnaire, one referring to nuns and the other to priests and brothers, asked which of eight characteristics the students had observed most frequently. The responses showed that 62 percent of the priests and brothers and 63 percent of the nuns were seen as dedicated, 53 percent of the priests and brothers and 67 percent of the nuns as honest, 50 percent of the priests and 64 percent of the nuns as understanding, 41 percent of the priests and 30 percent of the nuns as authoritarian, 30 percent of the priests and 15 percent of the nuns as out of touch, 15 percent of the priests and 12 percent of the nuns as phoney, 14 percent of the priests and 20 percent of the nuns as relevant, and only 7 percent of the priests and 6 percent of the nuns as unconcerned.

The contrast between these figures and the comments is most probably explained by the need felt by the students to sound off about those they disliked, even though they were perhaps isolated examples. Again, most of the teens were not able to choose the church they will attend and so were forced to accept — or tolerate — whatever is available.

The nuns, most of them in the schools, did not escape criticism:

> There are some nuns which are so rude and mean. They don't understand things about us. But the priests are so nice, sweet and friendly.
>
> Although not all my feelings for nuns are good, I don't stereotype them. It's just that in this school I've had more problems and conflicts with them than good experiences with them. Since most are older, I feel that they are still living in the world they were in when they left their life of being single.
>
> In my opinion, nuns are supposed to be kind, understanding and loving. They are supposed to be charitable. I find it hard to understand why some nuns are always so unfeeling. My (lay) religion teachers in the last two years have taught me more about myself and the church than the six years of classes with nuns.

One girl said that she found the changed styles of dress disturbing:

> We're getting used, in some cases, to priests out of uniform, but it's tough. When a nun says her cross, fish, flower pin is her habit, we are on guard. Of course, we try not to show it and if you confronted us with that we may or may not admit it.

Some Possible Solutions

The question is, what remedy can be found for the legitimate complaints? One answer could be in the greater use of retreats organized by the parish. Retreats were mentioned enthusiastically by a number of students. One said that they helped him because of their relaxed atmosphere, which allowed him to get closer to people and find himself.

The need for closeness and caring is an important key. These young people are not just alienated from the church; many seem to be alienated from the world. This could explain their not always happy involvement in sex, which seems to offer the ultimate closeness but which can prove a hollow sham without love and commitment.

The church, by helping them to a deeper understanding of God's love for them, can lead them to the one intimate relationship which will never fail them. But the church must be careful in going about this, for they are easily scared away, suspicious of snares set out to trap them.

As children of an affluent society, who take ownership of cars, stereos and computers for granted, they will not be held by social activities and secular entertainments. At best, these may draw them out of curiosity. Too many parishes, however, offer nothing at all:

> I think the Church has a significant role in our gen-

eration, but I don't think our generation is getting enough involved in it; it's not really doing anything to attract our generation's attention. In my church there isn't any youth group, nothing for the kids to get involved in. It's just the Mass every Sunday. That's all you can have.

One girl said that she had learned more from working with Special Education children than in her 12 years of religious education. They made her realize how thankful she should be and she saw retarded people as doing better than the average despite their limitations.

When asked what type of school they would someday choose for their own children, 34 percent of the respondents selected a parochial school; 11 percent a public school; and 48 percent a private school, no distinction being made on the questionnaire between Catholic or non-Catholic.

There are some encouraging examples, although they were not mentioned in this survey, of young people contributing their own time and talents to serve as youth ministers, taking responsibility for developing and running a variety of programs for their peers, and at the same time becoming active in the whole life of the parish. Ministries of this kind can be particularly effective in their outreach. Because they involve working with peers, problems of communication are reduced and the complexity of the parish community is better appreciated. There is less tendency to complain and more realization of the hard work involved in running a successful program when the responsibility rests with the participants.

The Prism program in the Archdiocese of Washington, which prepares young people as youth ministers and places them in parishes for a period of approximately two years, is one model. Another is the Echo retreat program, which is committed to making the parish community the center of spirituality for young people. A student who had taken part in it spoke with great enthusiasm of this program. Father Paul Lavin, who worked with the Echo program for many years, has said that it has helped young people "to crystallize their faith and (has given) them the encouragement and support to stay with the church when so many of their peers were dropping out."

Programs like RENEW also have the potential for revitalizing the entire parish and creating an atmosphere that will welcome teenagers and excite them with the realization of what the church can be.

Topics for Discussion

1. While it must be accepted that there is no "typical" parish, are there other ways in which communities can involve young people so that they feel a real membership and commitment?

2. Many parishes compartmentalize the generations. To what extent can young, old and middle-aged work together to become a more genuine parish family?

3. What can be done to stress to students and parents the value and importance of attending a Catholic school? Furthermore, how can this value be increased?

4. Could the Church get youth back by offering what Catholicism can do for them, rather than what they *must* do for Catholicism?

5. Is Mass too streamlined? Would resurrecting some of the pomp, circumstance and tradition capture youth's interest?

6. How can religion teachers convince students that their course is valuable?

9
VOCATIONS TO THE RELIGIOUS LIFE

> I would not think a nun is a bad thing to do with my life. It is just that I already have plans and one is to marry and raise a family. I do like the way that nuns can help people, though — that appeals to me.

Ninty-nine percent of the students completing the questionnaire responded to the question, "Do you have any interest in becoming a priest, nun, brother, minister? Why/why not?" and included explanations for their choice. This suggests a subject on which they had definite opinions. However, while they may have given the matter some thought, most had decided that the religious life was not for them.

Affirmative Responses

Five percent said that they were interested, including 11 non-Catholics who were probably thinking of non-Catholic forms of ministry. Of the 22 Catholics, 13 sounded as if they might be serious:

> They've got so much time to get closer to God. I'd

> like to wait a few years before being a nun; and if I do, I would be cloistered.
>
> I have worked in the parish rectory for four years now and I have observed the life-styles of the priests. I find the things they do interesting and highly satisfactory.
>
> I already went to a seminary high school in Pennsylvania for one year and found it interesting.

Others had more trouble in explaining their choice:

> I don't know exactly, it's just a feeling deep inside which pulls me and excites me whenever I think about it. I would love to be available to help people all or most of the time, and not have to worry about a job or kids I would have to raise. It is very difficult to explain.

There was also vagueness about what such a choice would involve:

> It's a beautiful thing to be able to serve God as a priest.
>
> I like working with people and seeing good done.

Two students said "yes" because they were "just open to anything," or wanted "to see what it's like, try something new," while a third added the proviso, "If I could marry I would become a priest." A young woman said that it seemed "a pleasant, nice life," but was not certain whether she could follow the same routine day after day, while a young man explained, "I've thought about it but changed my mind. I don't exactly know why I did, and it has never really occurred to me again."

It would, therefore, be too optimistic to accept the figure of 5 percent positive responses, as it appears that probably less

108 Faith Without Form

than half of that number would be likely to explore further the possibility of a religious life.

Negative Responses

These impressions are reinforced by an examination of the comments of those who responded either "no" or "no opinion":

a) 23 percent said that they want to marry and/or have children.

b) 14 percent would prefer a different life-style.

c) 13 percent were just not interested.

d) 10 percent felt that they could not make the commitment and meet other requirements.

e) 9 percent were negative, antagonistic or disagreed with church teachings.

f) 6 percent spoke of the need for a "call" and said that they had not received one.

g) 5 percent said that they could serve God just as well as lay people.

h) 4 percent felt that they were not sufficiently religious.

i) 3 percent had problems with the requirement of celibacy.

j) 3 percent did not know what they wanted to do.

k) 3 percent offered various other comments.

l) 2 percent had other specific goals.

m) 1 percent said that they had insufficient knowledge to form an opinion — an interesting figure, because the majority displayed very little understanding of the life of a priest, brother or nun on which to base their response.

These figures show that while 23 percent responded with

reasons that could be loosely grouped as "feelings of unworthiness" (items d, f, h, i), an almost equal number gave their hopes for marriage and a family as a reason (item a), and 43 percent were not interested for a variety of other reasons (items b, c, e, g, l). In other words, not only did those who answered "yes" make up a very small percentage of the whole, but the majority of the others had a generally negative responses to the whole idea of religious life.

This confirmed the impression that even in Catholic high schools students do not see the life of a priest or nun as something to be envied, but rather as something that calls for unacceptable sacrifices while offering little in return. There were exceptions:

> I admire them for what they do and I feel that it's great to give your life in service to God.
>
> I respect nuns and the way they devote their life to helping others, but that would be too hard for me to do.
>
> I respect the religious order because of their dedication, but at this point I could not make that commitment.

However, there were many more who felt that the life would be just too hard for them, that they could not "cope with the pressures of being a priest," because "the life is quite hard," and "I do not have the discipline for it." Some said that they could not even consider it because of the sins that they had committed. They seemed unconvinced of the existence of a loving and forgiving God, and had either not heard or missed the point of the stories of some of the great saints, whose early lives may have rivaled any present-day soap opera but who went on to found religious orders and to serve God with courage and conviction.

It seems that these students had little understanding of the real challenges of the religious life. They were ignorant of how brothers, priests and nuns actually live, of what is meant by a monastic, apostolic or cloistered life, of the tremendous work being done by many sisters, or of the opportunities provided by life in a rectory. They see priests, nuns and brothers in the context of the classroom or the parish church, and speak of their life as "boring," "doing the same thing day after day," characterized by a lack of freedom or excitement — as if the life of the average lay person did not also have its full share of routine tasks and responsibilities.

Religious Life vs. Marriage

The desire for marriage and family was very strong, and many said simply that this was the reason why they would not even consider a religious life. Some suggested that if it could be done, they would like to combine the two states:

> Some of the greatest people I've met have been brothers and priests, but right now I feel I want a family also.

> Because life in the ministry would not allow me to have a wife and children. A wife and children are very important to me.

Although none of the questions in the survey sought information on the students' expectations of married life, their explanations suggested that they had a much more hopeful attitude toward marriage:

> I want to be married . . . and learn what being a parent means and feeling really loved and needed.

> I want to get married and raise beautiful children like my parents have done.

> I think that you really miss out on something if you don't have a family of your own.
>
> I think my life would be more meaningful if I was to get married and have children. I would have a chance to watch my children grow the way I taught them — into mature, loving human beings.
>
> Because I want to get married and have a family of my own to bring up with love and understanding — also to bring them up believing in God because nowadays I see so many children who don't even know God at all! It's really sad.

These do not sound like romantic daydreams, but the result of lived experiences, whether in close, supportive families or in broken homes. One feels that here the students know what they are talking about.

While the desire for a family suggests the absence of the charism of celibacy, even if this was not mentioned directly, there were also students who spoke of this as a specific problem, including some who seemed to have little enthusiasm for marriage, like the young man who cheerfully announced, "I'm a person that believes in indulgence of the flesh." Others, both male and female, echoed a similar feeling: "Because I want to have women," "I would like to have a sexually active life," "You can't have girls and I think it would not be for me because it's not exciting enough; I like the luxuries in life, especially girls and making money," and "A celibate life would be too difficult." There were others who sounded somewhat regretful that they could not live up to such high ideals:

> I do not think I can live celibately or with little material goods. I often wish I could change my lust and greed for things of this world.
>
> Because I need to have someone to trust and help

me fulfill my dreams and someone who cares and needs me. I need someone to whom I can express my love.

Fifty percent of the questionnaire responses said that priests should be allowed to marry, although two students said that this would make them less effective:

> I don't think that priests should be married or that nuns should be married. If they are completely separate from modern society, they stand out with their belief in God and their love for God. I really don't think clergy should be married, because they would not seem so close to God.

> I don't think priests should be allowed to marry, because they wouldn't be able to devote their lives to God. There's the phrase that they are married to the church. If they want to be a priest, let them be a priest.

The "Call"

The idea of a clear vocation or "call" was mentioned by a total of 41 students, who said that they had not received it. Some sounded rather as if they were expecting a direct communication from heaven, one that would spell out the request without any ambiguity:

> Haven't been given a vision from God to do so.

> I believe God calls people for those positions, and as of yet I have not been called upon.

> Because Jesus doesn't want me to.

Others were more tentative about how this call might come, but were sure that they had not heard it yet:

> I feel that at this age I would have to have been inspired in some way, there would have to be a different personality.
>
> I don't believe that God has called me to preach his word to the people.
>
> At this point in my life I do not feel that it is the way for me to go, but who knows, maybe I will hear a call and respond.
>
> I have never been called. I think that kind of life takes a special person and God would choose you if he wants to. If I am called I still do not know if I would respond.
>
> I haven't had the calling to be a priest and feel God will tell those he wants to lead a vocational life.

It is perhaps worth mentioning that none of the students spoke of having prayed for divine guidance in choosing the life that they would follow. It was as if they felt that this was up to God — if he wanted them, he should let them know beyond any doubt that this was what they should do; if there was no signal, they assumed that they were not wanted and made other plans.

Unworthiness

The two groups who said that they were not sufficiently religious, that they didn't feel good enough or could not make the commitment, had much in common and totaled almost 14 percent of those responding. A number said that, not only were they not religious enough to make this their life's work, but that they were simply not religious, even to the extent of not believing in God. Some of the self-confessed atheists were not Catholic, but the confusion that exists in the church today was demonstrated by such responses from "practicing" Catholics as:

> I don't believe in God but I like religion. But you can't get married if you want to become a priest. I think that that is stupid. What's being married got to do with interfering with God? Is it going to make you a worse Christian?
>
> I don't like the life-style, but more than anything else I don't follow the worshipping of a God.
>
> I don't agree with the religious concept of a God.
>
> I don't really know if I believe in God. I pray to him when something good or bad has happened, and I also look up to him to give me strength, but I still don't know if I believe in him.
>
> I have a hard time understanding what is truly real about God, so I feel that becoming a nun is not a good idea.

Others said that, while religion was important to them, they did not think that they could be totally devoted to God. Here again, a common misapprehension was apparent. There appeared to be a belief that priests, brothers and nuns are expected to devote their lives, totally and completely, to God and think about nothing else, but that the lay world need pay attention to him for only short periods of time — usually for about an hour on Sunday morning — and that the rest of life can be taken up with more rewarding and interesting activities. This idea echoes a comment by Father Gary Bagley in an article "Is My Teen Normal?" which appeared in *Our Sunday Visitor* on April 4, 1984 (pp. 6-7):

> Young people have noticed that many adults are only concerned with their weekend obligation (and they know that adults want to occupy less than an hour of their weekend).

Vocation of the Laity

The students who said that they thought they could serve God as well or better as laity than as religious had grasped this point, but they made up only a little more than five percent of the whole.

Among those who said that they were not sufficiently religious, this separation of religion from everyday life appeared frequently:

> I believe in God and do what he wants, but do not want to spend all of my time devoted to him. I need time to just be myself. I know God can accept that fact.

> I do participate in religion, but I don't want to make it the focus point of my life.

> I couldn't sacrifice myself like that. My faith isn't that overpowering or even set firmly in my life. It just isn't for me.

> I could not give myself up completely. I love God a lot, but there is a better way.

> I'm afraid I could never devote my entire life to the church — perhaps I'm too selfish.

> I don't think I am that wrapped up in God to the point where I could devote my entire life to him like a priest or brother does.

Non-Catholic students made up almost a third of those who felt that they could serve God as well in other ways. Some were already "heavily involved" in their own churches or planned to become social workers, to do various kinds of volunteer work and to "witness to other people with the Bible and through my life. I don't have to become a nun to show them how God works in my life." Catholic students also felt that they could be more useful in other fields, some giving the impression that they thought this might be an easier option:

> I don't feel a need to make the commitments of a priest in order to be close to God or help other people.

> I really wouldn't mind if it wasn't for some of the rules and the studies they have to go through. If anyone feels he can contribute to humanity in some way without committing his whole life to it, then I might be one.

> I would like to serve the religious community, but not in a way that restricts my freedom to my own opinions and my own way of life.

Disillusionment

The mirror image of the notion that men and women religious must lead perfect lives appears in the comments from those who have noticed that they are human and have been disillusioned by their discovery. Some of their reactions are harsh:

> Many of the Church leaders at my old church are stuffed shirts. Turned me off from religious vocations.

> This may be from my bad experience, but I feel that many religious are a pious lot, most of them say one thing in their teaching and do the exact opposite. They justify these actions under the facade of saying "I'm only human."

> This is my 12th year in Catholic schools, being taught by nuns, and I have met many who did not fulfill my expectations.

> I am somewhat turned off from becoming a nun be-

> cause of the ways I have seen other nuns or ministers act when I felt their actions were not of God.
>
> They imitate God and think they have the right to perform his actions. And most become priests because it is a safe way of life. To me a priest should be old and wise; therefore they shouldn't get degrees (be ordained?) until about 35 years of age in my opinion.

The last remark evokes a hilarious picture of all those old, wise 35-year-olds looking for a safe refuge from the hardships of the world! These comments do, however, illustrate the very real problem faced by a Church in which religious authority figures, male and female, lead celibate lives that are clearly separated from those of their parishioners or students. They may appear to be either saints who defy emulation or hypocrites who are trying to hoodwink the laity. These responses show little tolerance or understanding of what is really involved in the religious life, as do the following: "I wouldn't enjoy myself praying and reading the Bible all the time," or "I feel that nuns do not really know what life is. All they do is pray. They don't face any of the hardships we do. They live a sheltered life."

Not all of those making negative comments put the blame on individuals. There were those who said that they did not agree with everything (or anything) that the Church teaches; others felt that it would be a boring life, while still others said that it was too restricted and lacking in freedom.

> It's a sad, lonely and non-beneficial life to live. It seems to me that if there turns out to be no God nor life after death, a whole lifetime has been thrown away.

Two specifically mentioned the fact that women cannot be priests:

> Because women are not allowed to be true ministers in the church because they can't be priests. I believe a woman can be just as good a priest as a man.
>
> Because nuns can't perform the Mass (usually (*sic*) done by the priest).

Fifty-one percent said that they thought the priesthood should be open to women, and one young woman spoke of her own frustrations:

> I've always wanted to be an altar girl. I used to memorize the Mass. I wanted to be a woman priest. I used to talk to the nuns across the street and ask them why they didn't have women priests. There was one woman I recall who wanted to be a priest but they wouldn't allow it. I used to take the book home and practice, get a little grape juice and a piece of bread. Sometimes if we didn't go to Mass on Sunday I would ask my mother and brother to sit and watch me.

Most of those who said that they would prefer a different life-style or that they were not interested in the religious life (26 percent) did not offer explanations. Some said that they "would not fit in," or "would not be able to fulfill my goals and expectations," or "I do not wish to practice religion as a profession." Others were more specific:

> Becoming a priest, nun or brother is not the life for me. I'm glad that there are such people. However, I think everyone should do what they are capable of doing the best.
>
> Because I want to party and to enjoy my life.
>
> Because I'm happy the way I am.

Vocations to Religious Life 119

> I've done things that a nun isn't supposed to do.
>
> When I think of being a priest, my mind goes blank.

There were three other small groups that did not fit in any of the major categories. These are the almost three percent who did not know what they wanted to do, those who said that they did not know enough about the religious life to make a decision, and those who can only be classified as "other."

Of those who did not know what they wanted, one commented:

> At this point, I'm confused about what I believe in. I'm not even sure about God. I mean there could be a race in the universe that is so technologically advanced that they appear to be preternatural like God and the angels.

Two others remarked:

> We never know our future, except God.
>
> If it is to be, so be it. God has a life planned for me.

Another, who apparently had some problem with the concept of free will, said:

> I don't believe that if he gave us free will he really cares how we act.

The unclassified answers covered a wide spectrum, from the reasonable — "Because I have not prepared myself for it yet," "I am not one to press my own feelings on someone else" — to those that echo the misunderstandings mentioned earlier:

> I have sinned too much to become a nun or minister.
>
> You act like just because I do volunteer work I am

going to devote my life, but that is a part-time thing for me.

I don't feel that I could be a nun because of the things that I do.

Conclusion

Although almost 14 percent of the students said that they would prefer a different life-style, only 2 percent cited specific goals. These included medicine, science, art, public service, professional baseball, nursing, business, engineering or architecture and politics. Medicine was well ahead, with six mentions to only two for engineering and one for each of the others.

These responses suggest another, more optimistic explanation for the small number who showed an interest in the religious life. At 17, these young people are still exploring themselves and their world and are not ready to make a final decision about their future career, although a considerable percentage are certain about their feeling that marriage and a family is something to be desired. Before Vatican II, some minor seminaries provided a sheltered environment which encouraged early commitment to the priestly life. Boys as young as 12 and 13 decided that they wanted to be priests and entered the seminary.

At the same time, the priesthood offered many visible advantages, including a secure future and a position of respect, leadership and authority which could be achieved by following the appointed paths with reasonable diligence. In the same way, the women's religious orders opened up careers in teaching and nursing, combined with security and status, at a time when women had many fewer career options than today. This is not to denigrate the many men and women who would have chosen the religious life then, as now, because of their deep religious convictions, but merely to suggest that the climate of the times has changed drastically and the young have more opportunity to judge the implications of a lifelong commitment to celibacy from their own experience as young (and frequently sexually active) adults. As one student said:

> I think that people may still want to go into religious life, but it would be with a different attitude from those who are in religious life now. The time, the age would influence them, because it is more fast paced now. There is more of a technological attitude.

The positive side to these changes is that those who do elect to follow a religious life today are more likely to have considered the pros and cons from a realistic, adult point of view.

Topics for Discussion

1. Has the need for religious vocations declined in today's society? If so, what forms of vocation or ministry could be developed in its place?

2. Are there practical steps that could be taken by parents or teachers to make the religious life more attractive to young people?

3. Is a married clergy an answer to the current vocational problem?

4. What does the future hold for the Church if the number of people entering the clergy continues to decline?

10
THE NON-CATHOLIC STUDENTS

I cannot understand what religion I wish to believe in. I've studied, visited and participated in religious activities from childhood to the present. I often go to different churches, hoping to find the right one. I want to fully understand God and what he wants me to do. I cannot do this without something to base my belief in — I am specifically referring to the church. So many times I have seen people involved with the church set bad examples for the youth of today. Without an accurate picture of the church and how we are to conduct ourselves as Christians or simply believers in God, the youth of today will continue to be alienated from the church.

Non-Catholic Participants

The non-Catholic students who participated in the study gave it a broader perspective, ranging as they did from committed Baptists to atheists and including a few members of non-Christian religions. There were also some from Catholic families who had either dropped out completely or moved to other churches.

Their special contribution came from their familiarity with Catholicism as they experienced it in school and their involvement in their own denominations.

Some spoke only of their personal religious experiences and their comments often echoed those of their Catholic peers:

> In the past year religion has grown to be very important in my life, a very stable part of my life. Though I don't attend church as often as I think I should, I don't think it makes me less religious. I have a very strong personal relationship with God, and church at times can help that but is not always necessary. I think the best way to serve God is by your service to others.
>
> I feel that I have a very strong religious background. I also believe in God and that one day I will die and go to heaven or God will come back for me and I will live forever with him.

A number of these teenagers spoke of the choices they had made:

> I was raised a Catholic until I was about 14 years old. I then changed to Pentecostal because I found that it met my spiritual needs more than Catholicism. I am now a charismatic Pentecostal.
>
> Even though I am not a Catholic I am still very active in my church and I do fear God, but that would not make me want to be priest or anything. I just try to live according to the ten commandments.
>
> Even though I go to a Catholic high school, I do not agree with many of the Catholic beliefs. I was raised Baptist and attended a Baptist grade and junior high school. I do not consider myself (part of) any religion.

> I don't think belonging to a particular religion is that important. I think a lot of people would be much happier if all their religion required of them was a firm belief in Jesus' death and resurrection.

Family Influence

Family members played significant roles for some students:

> My grandparents have been a big influence on me. I admire them very much. My grandfather is an elder (church officer), and my grandmother is a minister. When I visit them they talk to me about Christ and the Lord our Father. One thing about them is that they don't try to run my life nor my religious beliefs.

> I realize there is a great problem of apathy toward religion and God. I find this among my peers. I feel I have been blessed by having such good parents who showed me the way. Without them, I wouldn't be the way I am today. I think the only sure way for children to have a close relationship with Christ is through their parents. This is where it must start, then church. From the time a child is born, it should be taught about the love of Jesus and what he did for us. Then when the child grows up, he has a good background on Jesus and he can share it with others.

Others experienced, and rebelled against, parental pressure to attend services:

> At my house, I have to go to church. I think that is very wrong. A doubter in the community somehow lessens the experience for the others whether they know it or not. In my house, I can't discuss my confusion or views because they are so radically different than my parents, who are narrow-minded when it

comes to religion. My parents make snide remarks about my faith (or lack thereof) and it is offensive and hurtful. I am agnostic (for lack of a better word) and right now I admit it freely. Some day I may return to a church and religion, but it has to be my decision. What really turns me off is when people try to push me into making a decision which I feel I cannot adequately make at this time. Maybe the diocesan priests should devote a sermon to not forcing people to go to church. After all, we're supposed to have freedom of religion in this country. If the pastor of my church were to say, 'Let up,' then maybe my mother would listen.

In one instance, it was the parents who were reacting against this pressure, showing how long-lasting its effects can be:

I am not particularly religious because it was forced on my parents and they decided to let me do what I think is right. I wish there was a church that thought as I do, but I haven't found one — haven't looked too much, either. I was thinking about the Unitarians. I used to belong to them as a child and loved it.

Searching

There were others who were still searching:

God and being a good Christian is still very important to me. The main reason I've become alienated is because I'm not comfortable in any (church) I've found.

The difficulty in choosing between many denominations was mentioned:

I am at a very critical period in my life. I feel that

> believing in God is very difficult. I have to sort out many different religions and I have yet to find one that suits me. I do believe to some extent that God exists. To believe totally in the Lord is very hard for me. I guess you can say that I believe that there is a God, but I don't believe *in* God.

Their exploration of different denominations had led some teens to atheism or at least an almost total rejection of religion — not necessarily for adequate or valid reasons:

> The reason that I'm an atheist is that I was exposed to atheism and Catholicism and I found that when you are affiliated with any religious organization there are rules and regulations you are expected to follow. I don't like the idea of being told how to live and act and what is right and wrong. I also believe that religion manipulates people by telling them how it is or how it should be, and I don't like that either.

> I don't think religion is necessary at all to get in touch with God. People use religion as a crutch to say they are forgiven for their sins and then they ridicule and sin again. People only go to church because they think it is a necessity or routine tradition. I think that if you study God's word and love your neighbor and be good, one can develop a relationship with God.

Values

When it came to values, the responses of the Catholic and non-Catholic students differed very little:

> If I was rich, the first thing I would do is help the poor as much as I can. I feel helpless when I see a poor person dying of hunger, etc. But I do give to the

poor when I have and don't need the money.

I believe being a good person, living up to my own standards or goals, is more important than being religious.

They had definite opinions on sex:

I think that you should have sex before you marry. I think that you and your boy friend or girl friend should be really close and really love one another. But I don't think that you should have sex when you are 12 - 15, because you really don't know what you are doing. I also feel that birth control is a good method and the Catholics should not condemn women who take it.

Another girl found fault with the church's attitude toward sex, among other things:

Looking at the Catholic church as a non-Catholic, I see many things. Take confession. I don't think it's anybody's business what sins I have committed. That is between God and me. And about birth control and abortion: Catholics believe in natural family planning and I think that is a good way to get pregnant. About abortion, I think it should be legal in some cases. If you've noticed over the last couple of years, about women putting their babies in the trash and letting them die unwanted, I think the mother should have an abortion instead of carrying it for nine months and then literally throwing it away.

Views on Catholicism

The idea of confession created problems for several other students, for example:

> I would like to speak out against confession. I think it is humiliating. When you commit a sin, it is between you and God. You do not need to tell anyone about it. They can't do anything for you.
>
> In my personal opinion confession should just be between God and the confessor. From what I see, a person just tells another person (a priest) his sins. The only one that should matter is God.
>
> We must confess our sins to one another, but I recall that when I went to confession I got so little out of it. I find it hard to relate to, knowing that I can go to God himself for forgiveness. The priest seemed like a judge to me. I didn't like that at all.

Many of these students spoke of their feelings about attending a Catholic school, and their impressions ranged from positive to extremely negative. One said that he found more discipline and more caring among teachers than in public schools, while another spoke highly of the religion team which "provided relaxed give-and-take in a close community of friends." He thought that the church should use the team idea more often. Other generally supportive comments included:

> I feel that my school contributed a whole lot to what I believe in today. I feel that every child should go to some kind of religion class.
>
> I find my religion teacher most important because he is an inspiration.
>
> I think going to a Catholic school has not changed me for the better, but it has kept me on a good course.
>
> Religion has never been made extremely mandatory in our household. I really never went to church regular and more often than not never wanted to go. Since I started going to this school my attitude to-

> ward religion has changed a little bit, but I still believe one doesn't have to go to church to believe in God.
>
> Until last year, the fact that I've been attending Catholic school has not directly affected my spirituality. I have never professed to agree with the beliefs of the Catholic church. The last two religion classes I've had have helped me develop as a person and to mature, but as far as the school atmosphere, the sisters, etc., they really have not made me a better Christian. Most of that spiritual knowledge has come from my church background.

The last sentence of the above statement is a reminder that the schools cannot be expected to perform miracles. Some of the more critical statements may well have been made by students without strong religious backgrounds or those in a state of rebellion, who would naturally resist anything that they interpreted as proselytizing. They would not agree with the student who said:

> I like this Catholic school because the Catholic religion is not pushed on me. Although I don't think I would have liked to attend a Catholic grade school, I know many people who have changed their ways because of what happened to them in their younger years, the way they were treated.

Instead, their attitude more commonly was:

> Required religion classes in high school are a waste of time. If you want religion class, it should be up to you. The result would be more time for academic study.
>
> It seems like you are all fishing for students to be-

come priests or brothers or nuns.

I'm not saying that the brothers are prejudiced against other religions, it's just that they pump their religion up so high that if you're a Jew, Baptist, etc., you should switch religions. When we have a religion test, it is usually the Catholic concept of thinking. If you are not a Catholic you are in bad shape. They should teach something that everyone has in common, if they can, because it is hard learning the Catholic teachings and then practicing the Baptist way on Sunday.

There were several negative comments about nuns, based on the students' experiences in school and reflecting their high expectations:

I find that most nuns I know are miserable or don't come across as happy people. This might be why girls aren't interested in being nuns. If the sisters could show genuine love to students, they would be touched and realize that God is truly in their lives. Some sisters are angels, but some are not very Christ-like. They are supposed to be examples of Christ to the students. I realize no one is perfect, but the sisters have chosen this type of life. If they could be more loving instead of mean or impatient, the students would want to know their secret — the Lord. People are hungry for answers today, they need a way out, security, happiness and this is in Christ.

From the dealings I have had with Catholic nuns I have in a way become disenchanted with the church. Before attending a parochial school, I imagined someone who chose freely to give up their outside life for one in the church as a giving, open, forgiving person. Some of the nuns, however, are sneaky, rude, prejudiced and hypocritical at times, just like everybody else, and are only using the habit as a shield. They try to portray (themselves) as "holier than thou," when in reality they are sometimes worse than most lay people. I realize that the clergy are human and make mistakes, still I think a little "something extra" is rightfully expected from them.

Some of the nuns here pretend like they are so holy, yet they seem as though they don't care sometimes. They constantly argue and some are extremely impatient. They always tell you to be courteous and polite, yet they aren't always that way. I understand that they are human, but they should also practice what they preach.

Similar criticisms were directed to priests:

The clergy so often act holy, untouchable, unable to relate. If the religion of God is like that, then I don't want any part of it. I thank God that although I've been exposed to dead churches, to hypocrites, that I could see his love and still be on fire for him. He is alive.

There were a number of other comments on the Catholic church, varying in their degree of criticism but all valuable because of the students' special perspective. There is considerable truth in some of the things that they said:

I feel that the Catholic religion should be more rejoicing than it is. They don't let God into their life when they worship. The priests need to feel more of the Spirit than they do. The Catholics should let go, let loose, and let the Spirit take over.

It is a decade and a time of change. If the church is

not flexible enough to move with the times, it will be left behind. Personally I think the church is one large monolith which is too cumbersome. Power and wealth should be more evenly distributed. The hierarchical structure of the pope and other subordinates removes him from contact at the grass roots level.

I believe in all the churches. I am a Baptist and attend services every week. I also know about the Catholic church. I believe in it, but there are some things that should be allowed. They only allow Catholics to take holy communion. I believe that they should allow all baptized believers in Christ to take it. You want to help people and bring them into the church. Only God has the right to judge and say who can and who can't. They should also have some rhythm in there. In the Bible, God says to praise him through song and instrument. In the Catholic church this is not happening. We should praise with loud song and also they should clap and put feeling into the service.

I think that the Catholic church does do some good by helping the poor and underprivileged and I think that's great. But I was never wild about the idea of Catholic missionaries going into underdeveloped nations and converting people. People should be left alone to choose their own faith.

A Non-Christian Perspective

Perhaps the most interesting commentary was provided by a young Sikh, who had a particularly good opportunity to consider his Catholic school experience from the viewpoint of a very different religious background. In the course of his interview he made the following comments:

I feel that there is an eternal being, but that there is no need to have any structure. Each person has his own God, whatever he or she feels, the good personified.

I have found with most of the students here, in front of their parents and teachers, they'll say "I'm a Christian," but they don't really understand what Christianity is. If they don't understand, there's no way they can push it on me.

Young people don't see any reason to have theology, they just go to the classes and are very passive. If theology was not required in this school, I think only 10 or 20 percent would take it, and then only because they felt it was an easy class. They don't want to take it, but we have it every day. I can see their reaction — "Theology, time to go to sleep." I feel the same way, but I'm not a Christian.

Last year we had a morality class and every single issue was debated. A good percentage of the class was against the traditional Catholic view. They feel that premarital sex is OK. On abortion it was about half and half. The ones that were against it said that in the case of rape or some unusual circumstances like that, abortion was fine. There were very few that were totally against it.

Alcohol is rampant here. They say alcohol is a legal drug, and so it's fine with them. Young people try to act more mature than they are, and adults drink so they drink.

That's what I meant when I said that on the outside they are Catholic, but on the issues, they are nothing about what Jesus Christ talked about, as much as I understand it. Some of the students are Catholics but they're not even Christian. (They say) "Yea, I believe in Jesus. Let's go and get drunk tonight." It's that type of attitude — "I want to get to heaven, but let's do something else now." That's not Christian.

Somebody once said that the greatest Christian that ever lived, apart from Jesus Christ, was Mahatma Gandhi and that's the way I feel. That's the way a Christian is defined as being. Here it's every man for himself, the American dream. If you are in my way, I'll step on you because I want to get to the top. Everybody's caught up in the American dream, to reach their goals, have fun, live it up and worry about anything else tomorrow."

Conclusion

The primary goal of the Catholic high school is not to make converts, but to provide a living example to its non-Catholic students of what the church is and how its teachings are more than abstractions. From the evidence of this study it would appear that, while some schools have a beneficial influence, others are turning students against the church or confirming the negative impressions that they had picked up from other sources.

These non-Catholic students are just as disappointed as their Catholic peers when they find that there are indeed failures among the members of the church, particularly as these are represented by the priests, brothers and nuns who teach them. There are people out there who are eager for our help, as another student said:

> Kids want to relate, but they are turned off by the same old approach that has always been used. Kids are hungry and hurting to hear something good. God is the only true satisfaction there is. When Christ

rose from the dead, the veil was rent from top to bottom, showing that through Christ we could come boldly to the throne of God.

Topics for Discussion

1. To what extent are the comments of non-Catholics helpful in planning for the religious education of Catholic teenagers?

2. Would a formal approach to the leaders of other denominations be likely to produce new and helpful suggestions for parents and educators?

3. What effect does the melting pot of American religions have on young Catholics?

4. What value does exposure to other denominations and religions have on an individual?

5. How can Catholic youth be taught to be secure in and to defend their faith while respecting the beliefs of others?

11
CONCLUSIONS AND PROPOSALS

> A lot of kids know what the church says but they go against it anyway. A lot of it is peer pressure and a lot of them are insecure. Nobody wants to be rejected, so I guess they do it to be part of the group. They are questioning everything; they are confused and have a hard time making a decision. I think it's good to question before you make a decision, get all the possible answers, then you do what you think is best. Insecurity is a really big problem with young people.

Conclusions

Until now the voices of teenagers have rarely been heard. Books dealing with Catholic high school students have spoken *for* or *about* them, but not *through* them. The repeated comment of the interviewees, "Listen to me for an hour? No one's ever done that before!" stated perhaps not fact but honest perception. Unmistakably, the high school seniors expressed their appreciation for adults who showed seminal interest in their thoughts, beliefs, practices, fears, and desires. Hopefully, the results of the incisive listening will stimulate those who deal with youth to continue hearing them out, and to capitalize on their insights. This representative segment of seniors in the Catholic schools of one mid-Atlantic Archdiocese provided one fairly accurate exposé of youth alienation from the Church. It is hoped that the research, designed for replication, will be conducted in various other dioceses to obtain a broad data base for addressing the religious needs of youth.

Love of God, Problem of Church

While a superficial reading of their comments might suggest that the majority of these teenagers were completely alienated from religion and the Church, this is not the case. They had not turned their backs on God; instead they were intensely concerned.

Their desire to establish a loving relationship with God became apparent in their responses, which often included profound insights:

> Sometimes when things go wrong I think, "Where the heck is God?" Then something happens and you know that God was right there. He's not there to make every little thing go right, but when those things happen, that's when I feel spiritual, when I'm communicating with God.

Perhaps the greatest concern raised by the study may be the dichotomy between this ostensible love of God and the mistaken sense that the Church has little to offer in spiritual growth and in preparing for life in the world. "The search for transcendence and spirituality is apparent now, perhaps unexpectedly, among young Americans." (Fichter, 1985, p. 40)

There is no denying that today there are "signs of unrest and criticism," and that these are often most visible in families with an active involvement in the Church. These criticisms may

138 Faith Without Form

range from the dislike of change felt by traditional families to the unhappiness in more liberal families over the role of women or social justice questions, but none are lost on the children. They register the awareness that, according to their parents, everything that the institutional Church does is not automatically correct. This adds to the impatience they feel when asked to accept, without argument, premises that they suspect may also come under attack. Parents could lessen the risk of disenchantment if they made clear, for example, that criticism of Father Blank's homilies does not imply criticism of his other attributes, or of the parish or the Church as a whole.

When seen against the background of the pre-Vatican II Church, today's teenagers appear not only reasonable, but also strikingly honest and courageous. They express their opinions, ask their questions openly and expect genuine answers.

> I was brought up believing in the Catholic Church and in God, but within the past two years I've begun thinking, "What do I really believe?" I always believed what my parents believed, but lately I've been thinking, "Do I really believe in every single thing? Do I really understand what they are talking about and am I really involved?"

Although most of the respondents (89%) were born after the close of Vatican II (1965) and few seem cognizant of the documents, their comments represent amazing insights into some of the basic guidelines of the Council. These young people intuit the need in the Church for dialogue, participation, collegiality and strong relationships. They want to be consulted, to give input. Their comments denote a craving for community, fellowship, the substantial warmth of belonging. They sense, without question, the Holy Spirit's work in their hearts, and are looking for listeners. "We like to say what we think about the readings at Mass sometimes. We have other ideas besides those on sex, drugs, and alcohol."

The Role of the Family

The students realized that the family played an important role in their religious development, either positively or negatively:

> My parents always forced me to go to Mass. I hate it with a passion now.

> My parents don't know that I don't go to church now. I feel that I am old enough and am getting further and further away from the church and religion. If they would just let me be, maybe I would come back, but they won't listen and say that as long as I am living in their house, I have to go to church. I just sleep in church most of the time.

> I have been becoming very aware of a changing of attitude, as opposed to my family. I'm at a point where I can decide what I'm going to believe in. I'm not going to skip church, but my parents are very religious, and do I need religion as much as they do?

> I do what my parents say because usually they are right. They want me to go to church and so I go along, because I want to stay with the family. You get other people who just want to keep away from the family and do whatever their parents don't want them to do.

Loving support is most helpful at this time of searching and confusion, and the parents' own convictions generate more persuasion when not imposed on their children. Perhaps a better understanding of what the Sunday Eucharistic celebration means would result in youths' desire to participate.

The many facets to the home environment involve much more than attendance at Sunday Mass. A family conveys its beliefs by understanding and living its faith, and by being less concerned with the externals than with the inner motivation for actions. Those students who were able to learn from the family the meaning of forgiveness, thanksgiving, healing, service and commitment were also those who appeared to be most comfortable in their faith.

> Who more than parents begets the Church by communicating the good news to new members? . . . Parenting is not only one of the least dramatic forms of leadership in the Church; it is also one of the least appreciated. (Kress, 1985, p. 183)

A respondent's comment gives an about-face to the latter statement: "I think parents are the most wonderful people in the world."

The mobility of present-day families adds to their difficulties, because of less opportunity to become deeply rooted in a community. This was realized by the student who, having said that he felt comfortable in his parish, added that he had lived in the same neighborhood since he was five and had always attended Catholic schools.

The Role of the Parish

The patchy situation in the parishes ranges from those which provide little more than weekly Mass to those with active programs such as RENEW, plus regular discussions and education courses. Many students offered either direct or indirect suggestions about what they would like to see in their local church. The respondents proposed that the church get teenagers into small groups to attract their attention and give them a sense of responsibility. They asked for more activities in which they could be involved, more discussions on topics that concerned them and "more explanations":

> There is a uniform way of doing a Catholic service, I realize, but there's got to be more to give, something new and different. I think the Church lacks really dealing with new ideas. I hear nuclear arms talked about outside the church, but when you're at church you don't hear a lot about it and you should. If they want the support from the congregation, they need to face up to it.
>
> Usually the homilies have a relationship to my life and I can say, "That is the right thing to do. I was in that situation this week and I did the wrong thing, or I didn't do what this person did in the Bible. If I had, it would probably have come out right." Even if the story is from a long time ago, you can put it in your daily life and do something with it.
>
> I feel that the Mass is a bit too ceremonial. It just seems so structured that you feel you can't be a part of it.
>
> A lot of people don't realize what the Mass means, don't understand that they are supposed to be happy. Everybody is so quiet, being harangued by the priest. I don't think it should be that way. I've always liked the priests that can give you genuine examples.
>
> Recently we had Mass in my grandparents' apartment. It was less formal and very enjoyable. We didn't feel that darkness of the church.
>
> I like young priests. I can relate to them, probably because they understand teenagers. They don't go over my head.
>
> My parish is always asking for money and it is always for the parish. I think overall the church does a lot for the poor, especially in other nations, but there's

always more that can be done.

I haven't been to confession in a while. I had a bad experience the last time. I got a lecture from the priest and you would have thought I had committed mass murder. I was in the confessional box for half an hour and I got turned off.

There should be more participation by the people and more understanding. We have some charge of our own lives. Someday people my age and younger are going to be the parish. We will be active on the parish council and we could change things, talk to the pastor. That's what happened in Vatican II, wasn't it?

Although no survey question or interview cue asked about retreats, the students brought them up again and again, with enthusiasm.

As a kid I had a big fear of God, because a neighbor once told me that God could zap you at any time. In the Echo Weekend I encountered God for the first time as a mature, free adult. Since then God has made a difference in my life. The adults in the Echo follow-up really mean a lot to me and helped me. Since the Echo Weekend I have started going to church and have been getting a lot out of it.

When I went on a retreat we had Mass in a circle, with the priest in the middle, and that was nice. There were about twenty-five people and that made it interesting, because you could see everybody. The homily was more like a discussion; it got everybody involved, which was good. I don't know if I could ever see people doing it (in the parish). Most churches are so big and they have three or four Masses on Sunday, with so many people.

A non-Catholic compared his experience in different churches:

> When I go to the Baptist church the service moves me, you seem to be a part of the service. Then you come to the Catholic church and need toothpicks to hold your eyes open. I feel that when you go to church you should be able to bring something out with you. If you hear a sermon it should motivate you to do something. When I go to a Catholic church I find that I go in, I listen to the sermon, and ten minutes later I couldn't even tell you what the guy was talking about.

Generally these students showed eagerness to contribute, and they are at an age when problems serve as a challenge rather than a discouragement. Greater involvement would help them to understand the reasons for some of the things they now question, and at the same time enable them to contribute their own insights and suggestions.

The Role of the School

There will always be families that have little if any interest in religion and which do not offer children the experience of an authentic Catholic home life. These children especially depend upon their teachers, not only for instruction but for example, and it seems some are indeed finding this support:

> When I was in grade school we used to go to Mass once a week and the priest would talk to us. The religion classes that I have taken have given me a good idea of what's right and wrong. I wouldn't hesitate to talk things over with a priest, something like marriage or a job, or any moral decision, because from the experience I have had they are human be-

ings and there are some that I could really talk to.

Some of the non-Catholic students spoke of the experience of attending a Catholic school:

> I feel closer to the Catholic religion since I've been going to Catholic school. I've learned more about the Catholic religion than I know about my own religion.

> The reason I came to a Catholic school is because I didn't like going to the public schools in the area. I've thought about the religion for a while. I know a lot of Catholics and I'm not saying that Catholics are bad people, but those I know don't even practice what they are supposed to be living, which means that they must be missing something. I know a lot of Catholics who seem to be nonchalant or even keep quiet about their religion.

> Before I came in contact with nuns, I heard so many stories about people who got thrown across the desk. I used to see the television shows where the nuns would take sticks and slap the kids. Now I've got a totally different concept. They are normal people who have just devoted their lives to God. I think people aren't becoming nuns or priests because more of the emphasis is on success in life.

While these students learn about religion, they are still missing out on some of the basics needed now, and down the years, to help them answer new questions as they arise.

The Bishop

It would be tremendously worthwhile if bishops could meet more high school students on an informal basis, if only because these young people would then discover what still surprises many lay persons — bishops are people too! This might also effect better religious education than the present situation, where usually the only contact between the bishop and the teenager is Confirmation, scarcely a time for an open exchange of views. Learning the role of bishops in the modern world, their pastoral concerns, and personal lifestyles could speak to young people.

Youth Ministers

Some of the most important people working with teenagers are youth ministers, who now appear in more and more parishes, often as full-time, paid, professionally trained staff members. Because they themselves are usually young, they have fewer difficulties in communicating with teenagers whose concerns and lifestyles they understand and often share. One of the most rewarding "how-to" books, Michael Warren's *Youth and the Future of the Church,* (1982) deals with youth ministry and offers many practical suggestions. It stresses the need for a support community:

> All aspects of ministry converge on one reality: faithfulness to the way of Jesus. This way is to be embodied in a lived community, not just in books or in instructions to youth. To follow this line of reasoning is to see that the problem of youth ministry is not so much one of getting youth to come to church as it is of forming a community of Christians trying to move to ever greater faithfulness to the Gospel. (p. 1)

Time and again the students expressed their desire for dialogue. When given the opportunity, they were willing to talk frankly about their own experiences, particularly with sex, alcohol and drugs. Not all would be able to talk to their parents in this way, but might well open up to trustworthy priests, teachers or youth ministers. They are not so much turning their backs as banging on doors and trying to get someone to listen to them.

> We took a marriage course (in school) where we discussed things and everyone had their different view. It doesn't cause controversy or tension. Everyone's really interested. When you hear people talking you find that everyone believes differently. It's a really open thing and everyone accepts other people's opinions. It's beneficial to hear what everyone else believes, and then you can form your own opinion.

The Gaps

The data indicate the need for substantial content in religious education courses as well as further contact with spiritual persons in the home and at school. Church history deserves an important place in the curriculum to provide a firm background for Catholicism. Many of the respondents seem to be at loose ends about their religion. Solid theology is essential for high school seniors who hopefully will want to continue following its development through their college years and through life. In this meta-industrial, information age young people need to be strongly grounded in truth and discipline and have significant relationships with inspiring Christians.

"The concept of discipleship makes it clear that each member of the church is under personal obligation to appropriate the Spirit of Jesus", says Avery Dulles, noted Jesuit scholar. "Church membership, so conceived, is neither a passive acceptance of a list of doctrines, nor abject submission to a set of precepts, but rather the adventure of following Jesus in new and ever changing situations. The church may be viewed as a community of followers who support one another in the challenging task. Recognizing our dependence upon one another, we can correct what is faulty in the slogan, 'Jesus, yes; church, no', which aptly summarizes the attitude of many disenchanted

Christians. Were it not for the community of the disciples we would have no Scriptures, no sacraments, nor any other means of access to Jesus himself." (1982, p. 10)

A final requirement may be that nerve in teaching the faith that Cardinal Hume called for in an address to the National Conference of Priests for England and Wales, and which applies equally in the United States:

> There is undoubtedly an erosion of religious belief, a decline in religious practice. The prevailing atmosphere has its influence on our Catholic community and on our ministry. Would it be an exaggeration to say that since the Council there has been a loss of nerve on the part of many priests, teachers and parents when it comes to teaching the Faith? . . . There is no doubt that passing on the Faith in a world of unbelief makes the task of the modern catechist and of parents extraordinarily difficult.

All of us in the Catholic community who care for our faith need to pray for a renewal of that necessary nerve and courage, wisdom and understanding on the part of those involved with the young who are the Church of the future.

PROPOSALS

The following suggestions have resulted mainly from the research findings of this study. Data derived from other current investigations, and examination of successful religious education programs have also provided ideas.

General Proposals

1. Provide regular forums for listening to youth — getting to

the core of their insights, and incorporating feasible ones into Church programs.

2. Include strong courses on Church history in the high school religious education curriculum.

> Without some idea of this (Church) history we cannot understand the present condition of the Church as communication, and its leadership theory and practices.
> (Kress, 1985, p. 174)

3. Emphasize solid theology in the high school syllabus, and in homilies, retreats, etc.

4. Improve the quality of religious instruction rather than force religious education and practices on youth.

5. Clarify fundamental Catholic beliefs, and strengthen them by living example. Said one respondent echoing the stance of the majority; "Hang on; what you tell me to believe and what I see don't jive."

6. Promote a sense of community in the Church by highlighting relationships, personal growth, and the reality that "God is not a distant entity but rather a personal savior." (Vanderwall, 1985, p. 1)

7. Instead of demanding obedience without questions, give reasons when possible, and examples to convince youth of Christian values. Cite heroes and heroines (saints canonized or not) as role models.

8. Integrate the young into the Catholic community by having a youth minister on the parish staff, and a youth representative on the parish council.

9. Combat the materialistic atmosphere youth imbibe by stressing the value: what you are, not what you have or do.

Specific Proposals

1. Discuss emotions of anger, fear, love relative to all aspects of teenagers' lives, including God, religion, and responsibility for others.

2. Explain the meaning of the Mass and what happens in it in language youth understand. Recognize that youth generally equate the parish with the whole Church where they expect a sense of warmth, caring and celebration. Develop an understanding of the Eucharistic Liturgy as worship of the community gathered especially on Sundays to celebrate together.

3. Involve teenagers in the preparation of particular Liturgies for the whole parish, and occasional Liturgies for their own age group. Masses geared to youth could be rotated from parish to parish.

4. Arrange for home Masses at times of special commemorations to promote a sense of unity, freedom and openness.

5. Focus the parish homily on youth once each weekend or at all Masses one week a month, relating it to the world teens know as real, using their language and experiences.

6. Teach homilists how to capture a congregation's attention and relate Scripture to everyday contemporary living.

7. Note that the emerging generation of laity calls for a thorough and profound reeducation of the clergy — the young poignantly perceive this need.

8. Define the reality of sin as delineated in Scripture and Vatican II Church doctrines.

9. Clarify the meaning of conscience, and the responsibility for following one's *formed* and *informed* conscience.

10. Introduce the Sacrament of Reconciliation (Confession) later than second or third grade when children can better grasp its positive meaning. Schedule Confirmation at an older age, 18 years or later, when the young adult understands the commitment involved. Require the person's petition for the Sacrament.

11. Address the subjects of drunken driving and drug addiction through graphic movies followed by open discussion.

12. Approach the problems of premarital sex, birth control and abortion by psychological insights into the God-given life and nature of human beings; by talks from counselors experienced in these areas; by the tragic effects on teenagers' lives as concretely recounted by them, if appropriate at the time.

13. Reassess youth's need and desire for authority, attested by their flocking in significant numbers to cults where they claim to experience community, love, brotherhood. "The Unification Church appears to hold a special attraction for young Catholics." (Fichter, 1985, p. 25) When reminded of the Mystical Body as the church united in love, numerous teens responded: "Yes, but they (cult members) practice it."

14. Capitalize on the values of peer ministry under the direction of adult catechetical leaders and/or campus ministers.

15. Promote youth retreats partially organized by the young people with the retreat directors.

Conclusions & Proposals 151

16. Schedule faith nights monthly in schools or CCD groups on themes youth choose, e.g. forms of prayer. Provide an "ice breaker", input by adult leaders, pot luck supper, and small group discussions.

17. Follow up with a faith night for parents with students in Advent and Lent, using the same format.

18. Encourage further faith development in the home by providing guidance and support for parents, through courses, workshops, etc.

19. Allow youth to contribute to course offerings in the religious education curriculum within the school and CCD programs. Provide for some choices, while assuring that the basics are covered.

20. Budget some financial support in dioceses for Teens Encounter Christ (TEC) and/or similar groups.

21. Ensure the continuing spiritual as well as social values of the well founded CYC and CYO parish organizations.

22. Hold "speak outs" for youth and young adults regularly under the auspices of the Bishop's Pastoral Council. Analyze results for use by the clergy and other religious educators.

23. Suggest that church leaders address the increasing phenomenon of youth as well as mature Catholics remaining in the church on their own terms — rejecting the teaching on sexual morality and papal infallibility, while accepting the reality of God's love, the Mass and sacraments.

24. Use high tech/high touch along with symbol and story in religious education.

25. Expect the church to evolve with society in this meta-industrial, information age.

26. Utilize up-to-date research techniques to provide background data for all areas of ecclesiastical decision-making.

27. Promote an atmosphere in the home of appreciation for vocations to the priesthood and religious life. Start by pointing out that the clerical and religious life is a way of life, not a career.

28. Encourage church involvement in such organizations as MADD (Mothers Against Drunk Driving) and SADD (Students Against Driving Drunk). Social causes concern not merely economics and peace.

29. Design RCI (Rite of Christian Initiation) for the individual parish, taking into account the social and cultural aspects of the participants.

Appendix

QUESTIONNAIRE

This is not a test. You are asked to answer honestly, giving your own personal ideas or opinion. Please do not write your name. Anonymity is professionally assured. These questionnaires will be collected only by the researcher, and will not be seen by anyone in your school.

Please check ONE in each of the following sections — a little background about you.

1. Sex: Male (433); Female (342)

2. Age: 15 (3); 16 (53); 17 (635); 18 (87); 19 (3)

3. Race: Black (322); White (422); Other (34)

4. Approximate academic standing:
   Near top of class (272); About the middle (453); Lower section (54)

5. Last grade completed by your Father:
   Grade school (21); High school (226); Trade school (56); College (258); Post-college (161); Don't know (56)

6. Last grade completed by your Mother:
   Grade school (19); High school (277); Trade school (49); College (306); Post-college (96); Don't know (35)

7. Is your Father a Catholic? Yes (460); No (291); Don't know (26)

   Is your Mother a Catholic? Yes (547); No (233); Don't know (4)

154   Faith Without Form

Are you a Catholic yourself? Yes (565); No (201); Don't know (13)

8. Is your Father a *practicing* Catholic?
   Yes (322); No (102); Don't know (42)

   Is your Mother a *practicing* Catholic?
   Yes (448); No (75); Don't know (25)

   Are you a *practicing* Catholic yourself?
   Yes (424); No (107); Don't know (44)

9. Was your Grade School Catholic? Yes (532); No (251)

10. At present I live with:
    Mother and Father (572); Father only (18); Mother only (157); Grandparents (12); Uncles and aunts (11); Friends, not relatives (14) Other (0)

11. The chief wage earner in my home is:
    In business (office work, salesperson, etc.) (400)
    In day labor (construction work, street repair, etc.) (73)
    In professions (teacher, doctor, lawyer, etc.) (229)
    Other (specify) (70)

12. If there is anything else you would like to say about yourself, feel free to write it here.

13. Please indicate how important you feel each of the following is to you by circling the appropriate number. The higher the number, the more important you think it is, the lower the number the less important, e.g., 5 = extremely important, 1 = extremely unimportant.

	1	2	3	4	5
a. A nice home, car, and other belongings	11	42	272	270	188

b. Many friends	27	55	198	232	270
c. A lot of leisure time	27	126	321	225	82
d. A good family life	15	12	41	122	594
e. An interesting and enjoyable job	17	10	42	219	494
f. A high income	16	32	188	321	222
g. Freedom to do what I want	9	37	140	256	340
h. Helping people in need	10	30	143	289	312
i. Taking part in church-related activities	96	170	257	185	76
j. Going to Confession	194	193	208	98	71
k. Following God's will	36	42	165	205	330
l. Good physical health	9	10	44	195	526
m. A good self-image	11	14	56	187	516
n. An exciting, stimulating life	8	25	106	268	372
o. A sense of accomplishment and lasting contribution	10	17	82	250	419
p. Personal satisfaction or happiness	14	6	60	209	492
q. Acceptance by peers	52	95	236	248	148

14. What is your personal opinion on the following statements? Please check ONE for each statement.

	Agree	Disagree	No opinion
a. Sexual relations before marriage are wrong	162	521	98

b. Cheating in business is wrong	625	81	77
c. It's all right to get high on whiskey or beer if you don't injure yourself or anyone else	433	259	90
d. It's all right to take hard drugs (cocaine, PCP, Uppers and Downers) to relax and have a little fun	79	625	77
e. Mercy killing for people suffering from a terminal illness should be allowed	263	297	217
f. Abortions are wrong	412	248	116
g. Homosexuality is an acceptable lifestyle	234	385	161
h. Catholics are required to accept and do everything the Pope says	109	521	151
i. Most Catholics practice what they are taught by the church	236	409	134
j. People who practice artificial birth control can be good Catholics	523	93	165
k. A divorced person should not be allowed to go to Communion	17	711	54
l. The priesthood should be open to women	402	173	209

m. The church should take
an active stand against
such groups as the Nazi
Party, Communists,
and the KKK   474   167   140

n. The church should give
more financial assistance
to the poor   601   52   129

o. Priests should be allowed
to marry   359   186   237

p. The church should take
public stands on important
political issues such as
the nuclear arms race,
busing for school
integration, equal rights,
and the like   465   191   125

q. Most adults are hypocritical
in their religious beliefs
— that is, they say one
thing and do another   401   350   33

r. I should be allowed
to make my own decision
about belonging to the
church   743   14   25

15. Which of the groups below do you feel have been MOST IMPORTANT in teaching you about religion? (Check no more than TWO).

    a. Friends   (85)

    b. Parents   (448)

    c. Priests   (146)

    d. Religious teachers   (407)

    e. TV/radio religious
       programs (20)
    f. Newspapers/
       magazines (14)
    g. Mass, religious
       services (237)
    h. Grandparents (66)
    i. None (12)

16. How important is religion in your family? (Check ONE)
   a. Very important (272) b. Fairly important (450)
   c. Not at all important (59)

17. If you have children, what type of school would you choose for them? (Check ONE)
   a. Parochial (270) b. Public (84) c. Private (377)

18. Do you believe in God?
   a. Yes (722) b. No (17) c. No opinion (43)

19. Do you believe that God observes your actions, and rewards or punishes you for them?
   a. Yes (536) b. No (119) c. No opinion (125)

20. Do you believe that God has a plan for your life?
   a. Yes (513) b. No (149) c. No opinion (119)

21. Do you believe in a life after death?
   a. Yes (546) b. No (94) c. No opinion (142)

22. Do you ever pray?
   a. Yes (743) b. No (39)

23. If you answered Yes to No. 22, how often do you pray?

(Check ONE)
a. At least once a day (378) b. At least once a week (232)
c. At least once a month (117)

24. Do you belong to a prayer group?
    a. Yes (45) b. No (733)

25. If you answered No to No. 24, would you be interested in joining a prayer group?
    a. Yes (103) b. No (610)

26. Are you interested in teaching religion?
    a. Yes (126) b. No (535) c. No opinion (117)

27. How often do you attend church or religious services? (Check ONE)

    a. More than once a week   (38)
    b. Weekly   (406)
    c. Once or twice a month   (139)
    d. Less than once a month   (56)
    e. Mostly on religious holidays (106)
    f. Never   (30)

28. Do you read the Bible?

    a. Yes (333) b. No (438)

29. If you answered Yes to No. 28, how often do you read the Bible? (Check ONE)

    a. More than once a week   (454)*
    b. Weekly   (38)
    c. Once or twice a month   (38)
    d. Less than once a month   (107)
    e. Mostly on religious holidays (147)

    *this conflicts with answer to #28

160 Faith Without Form

30. How many times a month do you usually go to Communion?

None	(206)	Five times	(37)
Once	(165)	Six times	(8)
Twice	(76)	Seven times	(3)
Three times	(54)	Eight times	(3)
Four times	(31)	Nine times	(1)

31. When did you last go to Confession (Sacrament of Reconciliation)?
(Computer printout does not provide usable data.)

32. Do you think your parish programs are: (Check ONE)
a. Good (272) b. Fair (363) c. Poor (87)

33. Do you ever do volunteer work for your church or some other religious organization?
a. Yes (397) b. No (378)

34. Do you have any interest in becoming a priest, nun, brother, minister?
a. Yes (44) b. No (667) c. No opinion (69)

35. Why/why not?

36. The nuns I know are, in general: (Check no more than 5)

a. Honest and upfront	(529)	e. Relevant	(159)
b. Unconcerned	(47)	f. Phoney	(92)
c. Authoritarian	(234)	g. Out of touch	(121)
d. Dedicated	(494)	h. Understanding	(500)

37. The priests and brothers I know are, in general: (Check no

more than 5)

a. Honest and upfront	(414)	e. Relevant	(108)
b. Unconcerned	(55)	f. Phoney	(117)
c. Authoritarian	(322)	g. Out of touch	(234)
d. Dedicated	(484)	h. Understanding	(396)

38. How often have you done something you felt was seriously wrong?
    a. Often (113) b. Sometimes (351) c. Rarely (288)
    d. Never (20)

39. Has your idea of sin changed in the last four years?
    a. Yes (482) b. No (286)

40. If you answered Yes to No. 39, in what ways?

41. Are there many adults whose religious beliefs and example you admire?
    a. Yes (441) b. No (213) c. No opinion (116)

42. Do you have any other comments you would like to make?

*Figures not totaling 100% of population (784) indicate omissions by respondents.

Interview Guide

1. School _____
2. Interviewer _____
3. Interview Number _____
4. Date _____
5. Sex _____
6. Race _____
7. Academic Standing_____
8. Education of Parents_____
9. Religious Background_____
10. Occupation(s) of Parent(s)_____

(Cues)

GENERAL: Does God make a difference in how you live? Does God help give meaning to your life? What is God to you? How about the Church? Does it help you to know God and care about people?

Do you ever feel very angry toward God because of things that happen to you? What kind of things make you feel this way?

How important to you are: The Bible; Prayer; Going to Church? What Church activities are you involved in? How do *you* come to know God? What things that happen make God seem closer?

If you had a choice, what kind of church services would help you — would reach your age group?

BELIEFS/MORALITY: What are the most important things to you in life? What do you believe in most? What problems bother you most? Is the Church of any help? How can it help?

How do you feel about: Sex before marriage? Abortions? Mercy killing? Drug/alcohol use? Nuclear war? (Perhaps choose one of these to prompt)

What things do you feel most pressure about? Are there group activities that bring especially strong pressures? What are they? Do you often find a need to escape from some things (problems)? Have you found a way to do this? What problems? How do you escape?

Have you experienced injustice in your life? What about injustices experienced by other people? What does the future look like to you as far as justice for people is concerned?

Is there some way the Church can help in these matters — or meet your needs?

PERSONAL TRANSFORMATION: Do you ever have dreams or strong desires for the future? We see life moving and changing so fast these days — with computers and robots becoming so important. What helps give you hope for the future? Does the Church help? How could it help?

Do you find that life is just one big hassle — one thing after another with no time to think? Does the Church offer any opportunities for a retreat from this — help you find calm and peace?

What helps you most to cope with problems/tensions/pressures? When you have an evening free, what do you like to do? Do you have any suggestions that might help others to cope? What about suggestions for the Church regarding helping people?

STAGES OF FAITH: Do you find as you come to the end of

164 Faith Without Form

your teenage years that you have to make more decisions *on your own* about: Your faith in a Supreme Being? In other people? In yourself? Do you face more serious decisions that you have to make on your own? Are there ways the Church can prepare you for this?

What would you most like to see happen in this world as you look beyond your teenage years?

Do you think the Chuch is tolerant enough — of other cultures and faiths? Does it "hear" different people and listen to them? What can we do about this?

Bibliography

WORKS CITED

Bagley, Gary. "Is My Teen Normal?" *Our Sunday Visitor*. April 22, 1984.

DiGiacomo, James J., S.J. and Wakin, Edward. *Understanding Teenagers*. Allen, TX: Argus Communications, 1983.

Dulles, Avery R., S.J. *The Survival of Dogma*. Garden City, NJ: Doubleday and Co., 1971.

----------. *A Church to Believe In: Discipleship and the Dynamics of Freedom*. New York: Crossroad, 1982.

Fichter, Joseph. *The Holy Family of Father Moon*. Kansas City: Sheed and Ward, 1985.

Gallup Report No. 222. *Religion in America*. Princeton, New Jersey: March, 1984.

Hoge, Dean R. *Converts, Dropouts, Returnees*. Washington, DC: United States Catholic Conference, and New York: The Pilgrim Press, 1981.

Kress, Robert. *The Church: Communion, Sacrament, Communication*. New York: Mahwah, 1985.

Menninger, Karl. *Whatever Became of Sin?* New York: Hawthorne Publishing Co., 1973.

Potvin, Raymond H.; Hoge, Dean R.; and Nelsen, Hart M. *Religion and American Youth: with Emphasis on Catholic Adolescents and Young Adults*. Washington, DC: United States Catholic Conference, 1976.

Strommen, Merton. *Five Cries of Youth*. New York: Harper and Row, 1974.

The Word Among Us. (a guide to the Christian life, based on daily Mass readings), published monthly by the Mother of God Community, P.O. Box 3646, Washington, DC 20007.

United States Catholic Conference. *The Challenge of Peace: God's Promise and Our Response*. Washington, DC: United States Catholic Conference, 1983.

Vanderwall, Francis D., S.J. *Water in the Wilderness*. New York: Paulist Press, 1985.

Warren, Michael. *Youth and the Future of the Church: Ministry with Youth and Young Adults*. New York: Seabury Press, 1982.

OTHER WORKS CONSULTED

Brown, Marion E., and Marjorie G. Prentice. *Christian Education in the Year 2000.* Valley Forge, PA: Judson Press, 1984.

Chilson, Richard. *Full Christianity.* New York: Paulist Press, 1985.

Curran, Charles E. *Critical Concerns in Moral Theology.* Notre Dame, IN: University of Notre Dame Press, 1984.

Durkin, Mary G. and Andrew M. Greeley. *A Church to Come Home To.* Chicago: Thomas More Press, 1982.

Fee, Joan L. (et al.) *Young Catholics.* Los Angeles: Sadlier Publishing Co., 1981

Fowler, James W. *Becoming Adult, Becoming Christian.* San Francisco: Harper and Row, 1984.

Gilligan, Carol. *In a Different Voice.* Cambridge, MA: Harvard University Press, 1982.

Goswami, Amit and Maggie. *Cosmic Dancers: Exploring the Physics of Science Fiction.* New York: Harper and Row, 1983.

Greeley, Andrew M. and Mary G. Durkin. *How to Save the Catholic Church.* New York: Elisabeth Sifton Books, Viking, 1984.

McNulty, Frank J., ed. *Preaching Better.* New York: Paulist Press, 1985.

Tyrrell, Thomas J. *Urgent Longings: Reflections on the Experience of Infatuation, Human Intimacy, and Contemplative Love.* Whitinsville, MA: Affirmation Books, 1980.